THE RATE OF
EXCHANGE
AND THE
TERMS OF TRADE

DATE DUE

AUG 9 1985		
MAY 08 1992		
NOV 2 8 1994		
DEC 1 5 1994		
NOV 0 3 2003		
GAYLORD		PRINTED IN U.S.A.

THE RATE OF
EXCHANGE
AND THE
TERMS OF TRADE

S. A. Ożga

ALDINE PUBLISHING COMPANY/*Chicago*

First published 1967 by
ALDINE PUBLISHING COMPANY
320 West Adams Street
Chicago, Illinois 60606

George Weidenfeld & Nicolson Ltd, London

Library of Congress Catalog Card Number 67-25815

Printed in the United States of America

Contents

Preface

The study published in this volume has its origin in a course of lectures which I gave at the Université Internationale de Sciences Comparées at Luxembourg in September 1965. The invitation to give this course provided me with a motive to carry out large parts of the work. The book which is the result of it appears under the title of the course, and it follows the same pattern. Some of the details were also worked out at that time.

The text, however, which is now offered to the reader bears little resemblance to the lecture notes from which it derives. The whole material has been completely redrafted, new points have been added, and the scope of the analysis considerably expanded. In the preparation of this final draft I benefited a great deal from most helpful comments of Professor E. H. Phelps Brown and Professor I. F. Pearce, who very generously agreed to read the whole book and suggested many ways in which it could have been amplified and improved.

In the course of all these revisions the analysis has been carried a little further than it was originally attempted, and many details have been added to its algebraic parts. In spite of these amplifications, however, the text remains on the level of elementary economics, to be recommended to students whose interest in the subject is ahead of their technical equipment.

London School of Economics   S. A. OŻGA

THE RATE OF
EXCHANGE
AND THE
TERMS OF TRADE

I

The Subject Matter

THE subject matter of this book is described in its title and delimited by its size. It is an outline of the theory of the rate of exchange and of the terms of trade, concise in form and elementary in approach. As, however, these limitations may be interpreted in various ways, some preliminary discussion of the field which the book is expected to cover cannot be dispensed with if the scope and the purpose of the analysis offered in it is to be properly understood. In the course of this discussion some general relations may also be explained which are quite fundamental to the theory that follows.

1

The analysis belongs to the old tradition of conceptual, box-of-tools economics. It shows how complex phenomena can be split into component parts, and how the knowledge of the relations obtaining between the latter may be used to throw light on the nature and the origin of the former. The new tradition of economics is more concerned with proving theorems and testing hypotheses than with the provision of tools. This is an advance on the old, conceptual tradition. For only if we can prove or disprove a proposition, we know that it is, or is not, true; and only if we subject a hypothesis to a test, may we have some ground for the acceptance of it. The advance, however, is not so much in rank as in succession. It is not from something inferior to something superior; it is rather from something more elementary to more refined. For if propositions are to be proved

1

and hypotheses tested, they must first be formulated. The elements which go into them must be defined and possible relationships between them explored. The tools in the box of conceptual economics are thus needed to start the advance. And as the field is unknown and the progress uncertain they should never be discarded and abandoned on the move.

This is the first limitation of this book. The analysis which is given in it does not go beyond the stage of defining elementary concepts, and exploring possible relations between them. It is of a textbook type, with little stress on either proving or testing anything. The analysis could be developed further in the direction of either greater rigour or greater empirical content. This, however, would change completely the character of the book, and for this reason has not been attempted.

2

The second limitation is that of the scope of the analysis. It deals with one aspect only of the theory of international trade, with that of the ratios of exchange. Three kinds of ratios are relevant to it. (1) The ratio at which goods or services are being exchanged for money. This is simply the money price of exports, of imports, or of domestic goods. (2) ratio at which money of one country is being exchanged for money of another country, i.e. the rate of exchange. And (3) the ratio at which goods exported are being exchanged for goods imported, i.e. the terms of trade. The latter ratio is also often called the barter terms of trade, to distinguish it from the ratio at which productive resources of one country, embodied in its exports, are being exchanged for imports, or for the productive resources of another country embodied in these imports, the so-called single and double factorial terms of trade.[1] Economic theory, however, has little to say about the latter. It is, therefore, with the first three types of ratios only that we will be concerned here.

This stress on the ratios of exchange leaves out such otherwise

[1] A more detailed discussion of the various concepts of the terms of trade may be found in Viner [37] p. 319.

important aspects of the theory of international trade as the theory of comparative costs, of tariffs and customs unions, the welfare aspect of international division of labour, and the effect of trade on factor prices.[1]

The existence of tariffs and transport costs is neglected throughout. In spite of its textbook character this is, therefore, not just another textbook of international trade theory. It may, however, be a useful supplement to any of the existing ones. For just because of its focus on only one aspect of the theory little attention needs to be paid in it to the factors which are not directly relevant to it, and a more comprehensive study can be made of those which are within its scope.

To compare economic analysis to a chart on which only a general outline of a whole continent can be given and all the details of the coastline have to be neglected has already become a cliche. But this is exactly the objective which the present volume is expected to serve. By putting aside all details it attempts to expose the forces on which the actual level and the movements of the exchange ratios depend, not each of them taken separately, but as a comprehensive system, one always related to another.

3

The details put aside are of two types, those which are removed from the analysis by means of the *ceteris paribus* clause, and those which are disposed of by aggregation. An example of the former may be the effect on the world market prices of imports of a change in demand for them on the part of a small country. To focus attention on more relevant aspects of the theory, this effect may be neglected and the world market prices may be treated as constant. An example of details which are disposed of by aggregation may be the effect on demand for imports of a change in the distribution of income. If incomes appear in the theory in the aggregate only, the effect of a change in their distribution

[1] As an introduction to these other topics in the theory of international trade see Meade [19], Viner [36], Ożga [22] and [24]. Lipsey [12], Samuelson [30] and [31], Stolper and Samuelson [34], and Pearce and James [26].

is left out of account. The distinction between aggregation and the *ceteris paribus* clause is not as clear-cut as it may seem at first sight. For it is possible to argue that aggregation of incomes amounts to the same thing as the removal of changes in their distribution by means of the *ceteris paribus* clause. The distinction, however, has a certain didactic value. And in the analysis offered below it will not be difficult to identify the type of simplification to which the context actually refers.

The models used to analyse the factors which determine world market prices, the terms of trade and the rates of exchange differ one from another in the details which are removed from investigation either by the *ceteris paribus* clause or by aggregation. Some forms of the latter, however, are common if not to all than at least to many of them. Thus prices are always those of imports and of exports as a whole, and the terms of trade are the terms at which exports as a whole are being exchanged for imports as a whole. The rate of exchange is the rate at which home currency as one form of money can be exchanged for foreign currency as another form of money. In other words the theory is about the aggregates of all goods and services exported, of all goods and services imported, of all means of payment in home currency and of all means of payment in all foreign currencies. This usually implies that all foreign countries are also aggregated into one rest of the world.

These are the simplifications which will be also accepted in this book. They leave little scope for aggregation or disaggregation of the respective economies in other respects. Some scope, however, is still there. For even if all exports and all imports appear in the theory as aggregates, the national product may be treated as one or as several aggregates. If it is treated as one aggregate, the goods produced in the respective country must be identical with those which are exported from it. For what is exported must also be produced there. If national product is split into several aggregates, the theory may allow for the existence of goods and services competing with imports and for domestic goods which are not the subject of trade (like houses and roads). In the present essay some liberty will be

4

taken in either aggregating the whole national product into one homogeneous group, or in splitting it into exportables and importables,[1] or into exportables, importables and domestic goods according to which of these alternatives turns out to be most useful in the particular case.

This is, however, the only liberty that will be taken there in juggling with different forms of aggregation. In other respects the argument will be aggregative up to the extreme. No distinction will be made in it between different groups of buyers, nor between different types of income. It is merely through the application of the *ceteris paribus* clause at different points of the system that the model will be adapted to the requirements of the problem in hand.

4

To put the subject matter of the analysis in a more definite form, it may be useful to write down in symbols the main variables to which it refers. Let thus the quantity of exports and of imports be denoted by E and M respectively, and the price of exports and imports, expressed in the currency of the country of origin, by P and p respectively. The quantities E and M are aggregates. In the formal scheme of the theory all exports are supposed to consist of a single homogeneous good, and all imports of another homogeneous good. If the theory is applied to any actual situation, some index-numbers of the volume of goods actually exported and imported have to be substituted for the two homogeneous goods in the model. A difficulty then arises that the measures of the quantity of exports and of imports must depend on the method of compiling the index-numbers. The difficulty, however, belongs already to the field of the application of the theory, and not to that of the theory itself. It is common to all kinds of aggregation. No particular attention will, therefore, be paid to it in the theory expounded below.

The rate of exchange may be denoted by r. It is defined as the

[1] The terms have been introduced by Meade to distinguish the type of the goods from the goods actually exported or imported, see [16].

price of foreign currency in terms of home currency (i.e. a depreciation of home currency is equivalent to an increase in r). This is just the reciprocal of how the exchange rate is quoted in the United Kingdom. We will find it, however, convenient to define r that way. The value of exports in terms of home currency is then PE, and the value of imports in terms of home currency is rpM. The terms of trade are the price of imports in terms of exports and may be denoted by T. As the reciprocal of the price of a good in terms of money is the price of money in terms of the good, the terms of trade are simply the ratio of the money prices of imports and of exports. Thus

$$T \equiv \frac{rp}{P}$$

or
$$\frac{T}{r} \equiv \frac{p}{P} \qquad\qquad (A)$$

This is the most fundamental relation of our theory. For it is exactly these four exchange ratios that form its subject matter.

In the subsequent exposition of the theory the balance of trade will be defined not as an absolute difference between the values of exports and imports (which may be zero, positive or negative) but as a ratio of those values (equal, greater, or smaller than unity).[1] The definition relation becomes then

$$b \equiv \frac{PE}{rpM}$$

or
$$Tb \equiv \frac{E}{M} \qquad\qquad (B)$$

In the discussion of some aspects of the theory this formulation of the balance-of-trade relation is more useful than the conventional difference between the value of exports and of imports.

5

The most general question which a theory of international exchange ratios may be expected to answer is by what factors

---

[1] The same procedure is adopted by Black [2].

these ratios are determined. The insights gained in the analysis of this general question may then be used for a more practical purpose, to predict possible consequences of various forms of interference with those factors. Would, for instance, a devaluation of currency, brought about by government interference on the foreign exchange market, lead to an improvement or to a deterioration of the terms of trade? Would an increase in the general price level, brought about by monetary expansion, result in a fall or in a rise of the value of exports if there is no interference on the foreign exchange market? The answers to such questions are not easy to come by. They require not only some knowledge of general theory, but also information about facts, and – what is most important – a great deal of skill in putting the two together. None the less it is mainly to facilitate answers to such practical questions that the general theory has been devised.

The definitional relations formulated in the previous section do not take us very far in the analysis of the variables which appear in them. They take us, however, some way towards a clearer view of the nature of our enquiry. For if the subject matter of a theory is a ratio of exchange, the question which the theory is supposed to answer cannot be that of how the actual numerical value of that variable is determined. This can be made anything we like by a suitable adjustment of units. It is only in relation to some arbitrary units that the ratios which appear in (A) and (B) may be regarded as determined.

As the formulae are definitional identities, their validity does not depend on the choice of the units. But the individual ratios of the prices of exports and imports, P and p, may be given any arbitrary values by adjusting suitably the units of quantity or the units of money. The ratio of the terms of trade depends on the choice of the units of quantity. And the rate of exchange on the units of money. We have in fact four arbitrary units, two units of quantity and two units of money, which may be always so adjusted as to give quite arbitrary values to all the four ratios in (A) and (B). The only ratio that is independent of the choice of the units and cannot be given any arbitrary value is the balance of trade ratio b.

7

All this is pretty obvious as long as the quantities in the ratios are homogeneous money and homogeneous goods. In fact, however, the relations expressed in (A) and (B) apply to whole aggregates. Homogeneous goods are only formal representations of those aggregates. The question must thus arise what are the arbitrary units then? What is, for instance, the unit of exports as a whole or the unit of imports as a whole? No satisfactory answer can be given to this question within the context of pure theory. Some answer, however, has to be found if the quantity of an aggregate is to have any definite meaning.

The answer which we accept in our theory is that of statistical practice. In the actual records of exports and imports the quantities of the aggregates are usually given as index numbers. The quantity at one time (in one year for instance) is expressed as a percentage of the quantity at some other time (in another year). The latter quantity, that at the time accepted as the base, is then the arbitrary unit in which the quantities at all other times are expressed. As had been already pointed out the procedure is subject to the objection that there is no unique method of compiling such index numbers. The result of measurement depends not only on what actually happens to exports and imports but also on the choice of the method. Furthermore, the methods actually chosen may lead to inconsistent results, inconsistent with the relations expressed in (A) and (B). We will neglect, however, these complications. We will abstract in our theory from all problems of the actual measurement of the variables which appear in it.

6

A theory always requires a model: a system of relations which simulate the behaviour of the real world and are sufficient to determine all the relations which appear in them, subject to arbitrary values of the parameters on which the form of the relations depends. An ordinary system of supply and demand relations may be taken as an example. It constitutes a model in which the price and the quantity traded appear as variables, and incomes, tastes, prices of the factors of production, are the parameters. The condition of equilibrium (equality of supply and demand at a common price) permits us then to determine the price and the quantity traded subject to the given values of the parameters, and to trace the reactions of the former to an arbitrary change in the latter. An increase in incomes, for instance, results in a rightward shift of the curve of demand and leads to an increase in the price of the good and in the quantity traded.

The parameters of a model may be transformed into variables by means of additional relations. In the example given in the preceding paragraph, a relation may be postulated between the price of some factor of production on which the form of the curve of supply of the good depends and the quantity of the factor used. If this relation is included into the model, the price of the factor becomes a variable which is determined simultaneously with the price and the quantity of the good. It disappears from the list of parameters. Its place there is taken by the factors which determine the form of the additional relation. There must be always as many relations in the model as there are variables to be determined. For the model is, in fact, nothing else but a system of simultaneous equations; and the variables are the unknows of the system. And we know that if the number of equations is greater than the number of unknowns, the former are insufficient to determine uniquely the latter. The model is undetermined. If the number of the relations is greater than that of unknowns, the model is overdetermined. No solution can satisfy all the equations.

The more relations and variables is taken into account, the more comprehensive is the model in the sense that the greater is then the number of unknowns which are simultaneously determined and the more basic are the parameters. Thus a general equilibrium model in which all prices and quantities are variables determined by the parameters of tastes, techniques, and available productive resources, is more comprehensive than a partial equilibrium model of supply and demand in which the price and the quantity of one good only appear as variables, and all other prices are parameters. The more basic are the parameters the more reasonable it is to apply to them the *ceteris paribus* clause. It is more reasonable, for instance, to analyse the effect on the price of a good of a general sales tax on the assumption that tastes, techniques, and available productive resources are constant, than on the assumption that all other prices are constant. From the point of view of the realism of the *ceteris paribus* clause there is thus always some merit in making the models more comprehensive. On the other hand, however, there are also some disadvantages of making them so. For the more comprehensive is the model, the more information may be needed about the form of the relations in it to determine the direction in which any particular variable would move. In a simple supply and demand model the only information we need to determine the direction in which the price would change as a result of a rightward shift of the curve of demand is whether the supply curve slopes upwards or downwards. If, however, the price of some factor of production is also treated as variable, and the supply curve of that factor slopes upwards, then if the supply curve of the product (drawn on the assumption of constant prices of the factors) slopes downwards, we cannot say anything about the direction in which the price of the product would change. The positive and negative slopes of the two supply curves work in opposite directions, and we need much more information about the form of the curves to be able to say the effect of which of them would ultimately prevail. In some cases information of this kind can be obtained by econometric methods. In many others, however, it can only be guessed with respect to some actual situation. Not much can, therefore, be gained by making the model of a general theory more comprehensive if this entails that such information is then required.

More comprehensive models may be compared to automatic tools which do their work very efficiently indeed, provided only that they exactly fit the job. Simple supply and demand models are of the axe-and-hammer variety. They may be useful in a wide range of jobs, but they have to be supplemented with all sorts of hunches and guesses about what may happen to the parameters on which the answer depends; about what, for instance, may happen to the prices of the factors of production if the sales tax is reduced and output of the industry expands. The box of tools supplied in the present volume contains the axe-and-hammer models only. When using them great care must, therefore, be taken to give a judicious interpretation of the *ceteris paribus* clause. A parameter which is supposed to be constant in a model may not in fact be constant if the model is used as a tool to analyse an actual situation.

7

The choice of the model depends on the question which is to be answered. There is also some scope for personal judgement as to what is the most convenient tool. Some models, however, are quite unsuitable for some questions. Our identities (A) and (B) may then be of help in ruling them out.

Suppose, for instance that the question is about how a particular change in the circumstances would affect the terms of trade of a country if all the countries concerned are successful in maintaining the values of their respective currencies constant both internally and externally. Formulated in this general way the question is quite sensible. If, however, an attempt is made to tackle it by means of an aggregative model in which national outputs of the home country on one hand and of the rest of the world on the other are treated as homogeneous, it is precluded from investigation. For at that level of aggregation constant internal values of the currencies mean that P and p are constant, and constant external values mean that r is constant. Thus according to (A) the terms of trade must be constant as well. The question is precluded from investigation by the conditions of the model.

Alternatively, suppose that the question is about the effect on the volume of imports of a change in the volume of exports in the conditions of constant rates of exchange and of internal and external balance. A simple aggregative model of the preceeding paragraph could not cope with it because both b and T

11

would than have to be constant, and according to (B) the change of imports M and the change of exports E would have to be always equal one to the other. Such gross inconsistencies between the construction and the application of the model are easily detected if the model is sufficiently simple and its conditions clearly explained. These requirements, however, are not always satisfied.

The identities (A) and (B) may be also used as a framework on which the structural properties of the various models can be conveniently displayed. The factors on which the numerical values of the various ratios ultimately depend, may do their work through any of the ratios which appear in these identities. The models may thus differ only in what relations between the factors and the ratios they admit. It is possible, for instance, that the quantities and the money prices of exports and of imports are determined quite independently of the variables which appear on the left-hand side of (A) and (B). For a model of this kind to be determined either the rate of exchange r has to be fixed, or the balance of trade ratio b has to be equal to unity (or some other arbitrary figure). If both restrictions are imposed, that is to say if trade is supposed to be balanced and the rate of exchange fixed, the factors which determine the variables on the right-hand side of (A) and (B) cannot be independent of the variables on the left-hand side. Some of them must also be treated as variables of the model. For otherwise the model would be overdetermined. It is in the nature and the form of the relations between the respective variables that the various models of international trade differ one from another. The identities may, therefore, help to elucidate these differences and to compare the models.

II

Supply and Demand

IF a price is not arbitrarily fixed by law or by one of the parties in the transaction, the factors on which its level depends are those of supply and demand. As a further step in the analysis one may well ask what actually determines supply and demand. It is proper, however, to begin always with the first step. The present chapter will, therefore, deal with a straightforward supply and demand analysis of international trade.

1

The following technique has been used to show how the world market price and the quantity traded of a good are determined by the given conditions of supply and demand for it. The technique is usually applied to trade in a particular good, one of many on the side of imports or exports. It may, however, be also used in the case of whole aggregates of exports and imports. It is, therefore, with this latter possibility in mind that it is introduced here.

To begin with, suppose that the conditions of supply and demand for a single good are given in the form of the curves of supply and demand. Two pairs of such curves have to be taken into account; one for what may be called the home country, that from the point of view of which the whole situation is considered; the other for the rest of the world, i.e. all other countries taken together. The two pairs of curves may be drawn on two ordinary supply and demand diagrams and put together as in Fig. 1. The right-hand side of the figure is a supply and

13

demand diagram for the home country (denoted by H). The left-hand side is a similar diagram for the rest of the world (denoted by W). The quantities supplied and demanded are measured to the right from O in the home country and to the left from O in the rest of the world. Prices are measured along the vertical axis, in country H's currency on the right-hand side and in the rest of the world's currency on the left-hand side.

As long as the analysis applies to a market for one good only, no questions need be asked about what determines the form of these curves. They may be treated as given and independent of what happens on this particular market. The units of the scale and the relative positions of the two systems of curves are then determined by the given rate of exchange. Opposite one unit on the left-hand side of the vertical axis, there must be so many units on the right-hand side as can be exchanged for it. Thus if H's currency is suddenly devalued by 50 per cent, the scale of the diagram has to be so adjusted that twice as many units as before on the right-hand side correspond to one unit on the left-hand side, and the whole system of supply and demand curves on the right-hand side shifts downwards by 50 per cent in relation to that on the left-hand side.

If transport costs, tariffs, and all other costs of moving goods from one country to another are neglected, equilibrium requires that the same price is ruling on both markets, and the quantity supplied at that price by one market as exports is equal to the quantity demanded by the other market as imports. In other words, a horizontal line representing the price must be drawn across the diagram at such a level (at P in Fig. 1) that the excess of demand over supply in one country (in W in the figure) is equal to the excess of supply over demand in the other (in H). In the case on the diagram the equilibrium price is OP and the quantity exported from H and imported into W is $kl=KL$. This implies that $Ol+OL=Ok+OK$. Total supply is equal to total demand.

2

Supply and demand relation may further be combined into an

excess demand and excess supply relation. In this new form they give the same information and lead to the same equilibrium position as the original supply and demand curves from which they are derived. But they put this information in a form which for the purpose of an aggregative theory of international trade may turn out to be more convenient.

To give a diagramatical representation of the excess demand and the excess supply relations both sides of Fig. 1 must still be retained; they must, however, be used either of them for both countries, so that the respective graphs are superimposed. The excess demand relation is obtained by deducting the quantity supplied from the quantity demanded at each possible price. The excess supply relation is obtained by making the deduction the other way round. Thus in Fig. 2 DS represents the excess supply relation for country H, and sd represents the excess demand relation in the rest of the world. The former is derived from the right-hand side of Fig. 1 by plotting the distances between the supply curve and the demand curve along the horizontal axis in Fig. 2, to the right or to the left from O according to whether they are positive or negative. The latter is derived from the left-hand side of Fig. 1 by plotting in the same way the distances between the demand and the supply curves. The equilibrium price is OP, the same as in Fig. 1; and the quantity traded is OT the same as $kl=KL$ in Fig. 1.

A variable which it may be useful to derive from the supply and demand relations for a good is that of the demand for and the supply of foreign currency. In Fig. 2 the rectangle $OPET$ (equal to $kmnl=KMNL$ in Fig. 1) represents the value of goods traded, expressed either in terms of home currency if referred to the scale on the right-hand side of the vertical axis, or in terms of foreign currency if referred to the scale on the left-hand side. It represents, therefore, demand for country H's currency and supply of the rest of the world's currency. If the excess demand and excess supply curves in Fig. 2 intersected on the left-hand side of the diagram, so that in equilibrium the respective good was imported into home country H and exported from the rest of the world W, the rectangle inscribed under

15

the equilibrium point (now also on the left-hand side of the diagram) would represent supply of country H's currency and demand for the rest of the world's currency.

If the analysis refers to one good only, one of many which are subject to trade, the supply of or demand for foreign currency to which exports or imports of it give rise play only a very insignificant part on the foreign exchange market. If, however, the analysis is extended to all exports or all imports, the supply and demand for foreign currency which it helps to determine become a factor which may have a decisive influence on the rate of exchange.

3

The same technique may be applied to all exports and all imports in an aggregative model. As far as the technique is concerned, nothing more is needed than to give a different label to the quantities and the prices which are plotted along the axes. The quantities must now be some measure of the volume of all exports and all imports, and the prices must be money values per unit of those exports and imports. The problems involved in defining that unit have been already discussed in Chapter I.

The application of the technique to an aggregative model requires, however, a definite change in the use which is made of the supply and demand relations. For if all exports and all imports appear in the model, the conditions of particular equilibrium analysis are no longer satisfied. It is no longer legitimate to treat the supply and demand relations as if they were given and independent of the quantities and prices which they determine. The analysis becomes one of general equilibrium. A fall in the price of exports, for instance, may very easily result in a tendency to substitute exportables for importables, and in a downward shift of the demand curve for the latter. Similarly an increase in the volume of exports may have a multiplier effect on aggregate demand and may lead to a greater demand for imports. The analysis must thus be extended so as to take into account not only movements along the given supply and demand curves towards some equilibrium solution but also the concomitant shifts of those curves.

The shifts are due to changes in the parameters which determine the form of the relations. An aggregative model of international trade requires, therefore, that these parameters may have to be transformed into variables by means of additional relations. What variables are to be introduced and what relations between them are to be considered depends usually on the purpose which the model is supposed to serve. The technique of supply and demand curves may still be used as a tool of analysis. The possibility, however, of a change in the parameters on which this form depends must be taken into account.

4

In the theory of consumer demand the quantity of a consumer good demanded is usually regarded as a function of the price of the good, of the prices of other goods, of the consumer's income, and of his tastes. The prices and the income appear as independent variables, and the tastes determine the form of the function. It may thus be argued by analogy that the shortest list of the parameters which determine the form of the demand curves for exportables and importables in an aggregative model should include the prices of importables and exportables respectively and the level of aggregate spending. The latter is often called absorption. The quantity demanded may then be written as follows

$$D_e = D_e(P, rp, A)$$

and $$D_m = D_m(P, rp, A) \qquad\qquad \text{(C)}$$

Absorption is here denoted by A and the prices of exports and imports by P and rp respectively. The tastes do not appear as a variable. They are taken into account in the form of the functions D_e and D_m. If there are also domestic goods in the model, their price must be added to the list of the parameters on the right-hand side.

The analysis of consumer demand, however, cannot be

applied to whole aggregates of exportables and importables without reservations. In the first place the aggregative character of the variable A must also be emphasised. The possibility of its being distributed in various ways between different consumers does not arise because no individual consumers appear in the model. The demand functions apply to the economy as a whole, treated as one consumer with given and constant tastes. In fact, however, the form of the functions does depend on how absorption is distributed between people with different tastes.

It must be further borne in mind that the aggregates of exports and of imports consist not only of consumer goods but also of raw materials and capital goods. The form of the demand function must, therefore, depend not only on the behaviour of the consumers but also on that of firms. The difficulty may then arise that if raw materials are imported and consumer goods exported, the form of the demand function for the former may depend on the output of the latter. Demand for raw materials might thus change in that case as a result of a change in total output of consumer goods, brought about by a change in the demand for them abroad, even if tastes, techniques, prices and aggregate absorption remained unchanged. To allow for this possibility the list of the variables which appear in the demand functions would have to be extended to cover also the quantities of the goods produced.

Finally, absorption is treated here as equivalent to income in the theory of consumer demand. In fact, however, even if the demand functions in (C) applied to consumers only, the level of aggregate spending A might not be as independent of prices P and rp as income is usually supposed to be. For a change in the price of a good may easily lead to a change in total spending out of the same income, the balance being saved or dissaved. Furthermore, total spending may be related to money balances actually held which in turn may depend on past trends in the balance of payments.[1] It may be argued, therefore, that absorption is not only a parameter which determines the flow of trade

---

[1] This is one of the main features of the international trade model constructed by Kemp [6].

through supply and demand relations, but it is also a variable which itself depends on that trade.

However, to make our analysis simple the complications mentioned above will be neglected. The quantity demanded of exportables and importables will be treated as uniquely determined by the prices and by aggregate absorption. The usual distinction may then be made between the income effect and the substitution effect of changes in these variables. If absorption increases and prices remain constant, demand increases on account of the income effect. If one of the prices falls, the other prices and absorption remaining constant, the good the price of which has fallen tends to be substituted for the other goods. At the same time more of each of the goods can be obtained by spending on them the same total amount of money as before. The quantity demanded of the cheaper good tends thus to increase on account of both the income and the substitution effect, and the quantity of other goods tends to increase on account of the income effect and to decrease on account of the substitution effect. In the analysis given in this volume, no questions will be asked about whether the two effects are in consumption or in production. In an aggregative analysis in which all sorts of goods have to be put together into very broad categories of exportables and importables there is not much room for a distinction between consumer and producer goods.

5

In the analysis of individual markets demand relations on one market are treated as independent of what is happening on the others. Can the same be the case in an aggregative analysis? The cross effects between the markets may be taken into account by all prices being included in all demand relations. The quantities demanded are then related to the same variables in each case. The fact, however, that all goods are segregated into a very small number of aggregates may impose restrictions on the form of these relations.

If the goods are segregated into two categories only, those

of exportables and importables, the form of one relation imposes quite definite restriction on the form of the other. For the part of absorption which is not intended to be spent on exportables must be intended to be spent on importables. Thus if the first function in (C) determines D_e in relation to given P, rp and A, it determines also the amount of absorption which is intended to be spent on exportables. The residual of A which is going to be spent on importables, and in consequence the quantity of the latter, are then determined as well. The form of the relation D_m can, therefore, be derived from the form of D_e.

It follows that a movement along one relation implies a shift of the other. For if as a result of a *ceteris paribus* change in the price of exportables a greater or a small proportion of absorption is spent on them, a smaller or a greater proportion of absorption must also be spent on importables, and a smaller or a greater quantity of the latter must be demanded. The only case in which no change in demand for importables would occur is that of the elasticity of demand for exportables being equal to unity. The same argument applies *mutatis mutandis* to the effect on the form of the demand relation for exportables of a movement along the relation for importables.

This mutual interdependence of the form and position of the two curves of demand derives from the fact that in a two-commodity-model the aggregate absorption has to be completely exhausted by the demand for the two goods. The interdependence cannot, therefore, be assumed away in that case by means of the *ceteris paribus* clause. The situation is different if goods and services are segregated into more than two groups. If to exportables and importables are also added domestic goods, like houses and haircuts which cannot be either exported or imported from abroad, two new variables must be introduced into the system: the price and the quantity of those goods. The demand functions become then

$$D_e = D_e (P, rp, \pi, A)$$
$$D_m = D_m (P, rp, \pi, A)$$
$$D_a = D_a (P, rp, \pi, A)$$

20

where π is the price of domestic goods. One of these relations is determined by the other two. The two, however, can be treated as independent one of the other, and no logical inconsistency would arise if the relations for exportables and importables were chosen as those to which this condition applies.

6

The form of a supply function is determined by the prices of the factors of production and by the conditions of technique. The firms are supposed to maximize their profits. To produce any given quantity of output they choose, therefore, that combination of the factors which in the given condition of technique and at the given prices of the factors costs less than any other; and they expand their outputs up to that level at which the additional cost of one more unit of output is just equal to the price which can be obtained for that unit.

To make our analysis simple, and yet not lose track of any of the relations which may be relevant to it, the factors which are used in the production of the aggregates in the model may also be aggregated into groups. One of them will be called labour. It is supposed to be used in the production of all types of goods. The price of it will be denoted by w and will appear as an explicit parameter in the supply functions of all the aggregates. The other factors will be treated as specific to the respective industries, and their existence will be taken into account in the form of the supply relations. The latter may thus be written (for country H) as

$$S_e = S_e (P, w)$$
$$S_m = S_m (rp, w) \qquad \text{(D)}$$
$$S_d = S_d (\pi, w)$$

No joint production is allowed for. The price of one aggregative good only appears, therefore, in each relation.

The complication of the relations being interdependent does not arise in this case. For the only thing that binds the supply of various goods together is the available supply of labour. This, however, does not appear in the relations at all. It does its work through w. Owing to a limited supply of labour it may not be possible to move freely along the supply curves for different goods without affecting the level of wages and, in consequence, the position and form of the curves themselves. This does not mean, however, that the quantity supplied of one good is determined by the supply relation for some other good. Even if two aggregates only are considered, the relations may be treated as independent one of the other. For either of them is constructed on the assumption that the necessary amount of labour can be always obtained at the current wage.

7

As a crude approximation to the actual conditions, simple theoretical models of international trade are often constructed on the assumption that the supply and demand relations are given and constant not only for individual goods but also for the aggregates of exportables and importables. Consistency of this assumption with the principles of economic theory is usually achieved by imposing restrictions on the applicability of the model to actual situations.

One possibility is to make the model applicable to these cases only in which income derived from production of exportables and importables, and expenditure on exportables and importables are very small in relation to total national income and total absorption. What happens on the respective markets has then very little effect on A, on w, and on π. Furthermore, if exportables and importables are not close substitutes one for the other in consumption and in production, the cross effects on supply and demand for them of changes in each other's prices must also be very small. Thus the supply and demand relations for exportables and importables may be treated as virtually constant and independent one of the other.

Another possibility is to treat absorption and wages as determined by considerations of domestic policy which have nothing to do with international trade. Even, therefore, if some tendencies in the latter may have an effect on A and w, the effect is offset by policy measures designed to keep these two parameters constant. What may then change are prices only. As, however, the cross effects of changes in prices consist of substitution and income effects working in opposite directions, they are not likely to be strong (and their direction is uncertain). Again, therefore, the supply and demand relations may be accepted as given and treated as virtually independent one from the other.

The cross effects may further be disposed of by means of additional assumptions about the form of specialisation in trade. It has, for instance, been assumed in a model constructed by Black [2] that exportables are not consumed in the exporting country, and that the price of domestic goods is always kept constant. This means that the only prices which appear in the supply and demand relations are the price of exportables in the supply relation and the price of importables in the demand relation. All cross effects are thus completely assumed away.

It has been noted already in the preceding chapter that a very common simplification of international trade models is to treat all home-produced goods as one aggregate and neglect the existence of industries supplying importables. The assumption is much less objectionable than it may seem at first sight. For it must be remembered that goods and services may be usefully aggregated not only if they are substitutes one for another on the side of demand, but also if they are substitutes on the side of supply. If, therefore, imports compete with a very wide range of home-produced goods (as in more advanced economies they certainly do), the possibility of producing one kind of the latter instead of another may in fact be the only basis for any aggregation at all. From the point of view of the supply and demand analysis the procedure is very useful. For (as will be explained in more detail later on) it enables us to identify the condition of internal balance of a country with a constant and perfectly elastic curve of supply of exportables.

On the whole the restrictions imposed on the applicability of the model by the conditions discussed in this section are quite severe. For it is not easy to find a situation in which any of them would really be satisfied. There is no doubt that an analysis of any of the major events in the recent history of the world economy would be grossly misleading if it was based on the assumption that the general level of wages is constant or that aggregate spending is independent of international trade. In the remaining parts of this book, we will thus have to consider more carefully the possibility of turning some of the parameters of the supply and demand model into dependent variables. Whether this is better done by introducing into it additional relations and making the model more comprehensive, or by letting some of its ends remain open and leaving it to those who are going to use the model to link them up as well as they can when they are confronted with an actual situation, is a matter for judgement. We will have the opportunity to proceed in both these directions.

III

The Value of Money Effect
and the Trade Effect

IF the technique of supply and demand is applied to an aggregative model of international trade, two sets of relations must be taken into account. The price and volume of imports is determined by the relations of supply and demand for importables in the home country and abroad; and the price and volume of exports is determined by similar relations for exportables. These two sets of relations are connected one with the other through the variables which determine the form of the respective functions and the equilibrium positions of the two markets. There is nothing, however, in the technique that would also ensure equilibrium on the market for foreign exchange. Equilibrium of supply and demand for imports and for exports does not imply that the values of imports and of exports are equal one to the other or to a given balance on capital account. In terms of the identities (A) and (B) the situation may be described as one in which the right-hand side variables in them are determined by factors which do not appear on the left-hand side. Both the terms of trade T and the balance of trade ratio b are determined by what these right-hand side variables happen to be and by the rate of exchange. No mechanism is implied in the supply and demand relations for the balance of payments to be in equilibrium.

It may be argued, however, that the balance of payments cannot remain in disequilibrium for long. For sooner or later the foreign exchange reserves of the deficit country would then

25

become exhausted. Over longer periods of time the ratio b must, therefore, be such as to preclude this possibility. It cannot then be a variable of the model. It is determined by the condition that foreign exchange reserves must not become exhausted. If, however, the model is not to become overdetermined, other variables must be introduced into it, and some other relations to link them up with those which are already there. These may be either the rate of exchange and the condition of equilibrium of supply and demand on the foreign exchange market; or some factors which influence the form of the supply and demand functions for exports and imports. The present and the next chapters will deal with the second alternative. The first will be considered in Chapter V.

1

The possibility to be taken into account first is that the balance of payments is affected by random factors which sometimes work in one direction, sometimes in the other. Over a certain period of time their effect on the balance of payments may thus cancel out, and if sufficient reserves of foreign exchange are available, no mechanism may be required to keep it in equilibrium. If something extraordinary happens, or there is some accidental accumulation of disturbances all of them working in one direction, some steps may have to be taken to put the matters right. These, however, would be more in the nature of emergency measures, determined by the requirements and the specific conditions of the actual situation, than systematic adjustments of the model. In the model the balance of trade ratio would be a constant.

An example of an emergency measure may be a foreign loan. The gap in the balance of payments is then closed by an item which has nothing to do with trade. It is possible that before the proceeds from the loan become exhausted the balance of trade will improve owing to random factors working now in the opposite direction, and no adjustments in the factors which determine supply and demand for exports and imports will be necessary. When after some time a new emergency arises, the situation may be quite different. A foreign loan may not be obtainable, or the government may be predisposed against borrowing abroad on grounds of principle; and the deficit may have to be dealt with by import restrictions or exchange control. In a world of this kind equilibrium of the balance of payments would be simply a result of a historical process in which one phase is never like another, and one form of adjustment never like another form.

This interpretation of the actual working of the world's economy is by no means implausible. Few theorists, however, would be satisfied with it as a condition of a model. For what it amounts to is, in fact, that over long periods of time the model is overdetermined, and that it breaks down and has to be mended when the stress of events becomes too strong.

2

In theoretical analysis equilibrium of the balance of payment is often identified with equilibrium of the balance of trade. The whole capital account is then neglected. The purpose is to make the model simple. Very little in fact can be said about capital movements in general terms. They are determined by expectations of profits, confidence in political stability and economic viability of the countries concerned, by political considerations of the government, etc.; by those factors in other words which in a theory are usually abstracted from. To make capital movements a dependent variable we would need not only a more complicated theory but also a different one, different from that which has been developed in the other fields of the discipline.

This does not mean that the capital amount of the balance of payments must be completely assumed away. It only means that the most convenient way of its being included into the model is not as a variable but as a parameter. The mechanism through which equilibrium of the balance of payments is supposed to be maintained must simply be such that through adjustments in the rate of exchange or in supply and demand conditions for exports and imports the balance on current account is brought into equilibrium with the given balance on capital account. All questions about possible adjustments in the balance on capital account to changes in any of the variables which appear in the model are then precluded. This price, however, has to be paid for bringing in the capital account at all. For on the level of abstraction of an elementary theory no simple and plausible relations can be assumed to exist between capital movements on one hand and any of the factors which determine the flow of trade on the other.[1]

3

A possible mechanism through which equilibrium of the balance of payments may be maintained is that of adjustments in the general price level in response to changes in the quantity of money. This is the classical theory of international payments under the gold standard. In terms of the model of the preceding chapter, the adjustments imply shifts of the supply and demand schedules, due to changes in prices, in money wages, and in aggregate absorption. The parameters on which the form of the schedules depends become the model's variables. In the country with a deficit in its balance of payments, reserves of gold and foreign exchange decrease, the quantity of money becomes smaller, aggregate absorption declines in money terms, and money wages and prices fall. In the country with a surplus in its balance of payments, the quantity of money, prices, money wages, and absorption increase. The rate of exchange remains constant throughout, determined by the gold content of the respective currencies. Thus the supply and demand curves in the deficit country shift downwards and those in the surplus country shift upwards.

If aggregation is in terms of exportables, importables, and domestic goods, nothing definite can be said about the shifts of the curves. At first sight one might think that in accordance

[1] Some difficulties may appear if a given balance on capital account to which the balance of trade has to adjust itself is interpreted as a given ratio b. For a constant b (if not equal to unity) does not necessarily mean that the absolute amount of the balance of trade is constant. This point, however, will be neglected.

with the quantity theory of money, prices, absorption, and wages should change all of them in the same proportion as the quantity of money, and that the supply and demand curves should shift in that proportion as well. In fact, however, this is not so. A glance at Fig. 1 will suffice to see that in an international trade model all money values cannot change in the same proportion. For, if the price of the good to which the figure refers fell in the same proportion as absorption and prices of other goods in country H, it could not at the same time increase in the rest of the world W. The same is true for goods which are exported from W and imported in H. Some changes in relative prices are bound to occur, and they must affect the position of the supply and demand curves. Not only, therefore, the adjustments in prices are determined by the shifts in the supply and demand curves, but the shifts depend also on the adjustments in prices.

There is further the question of how in fact changes in absorption, brought about by changes in the quantity of money, affect wages. A fall in absorption in the deficit country H reduces demand for goods produced in H; an increase in absorption in the rest of the world increases demand for the goods produced in H. And there is nothing in the relations on which these movements depend that would make the aggregate demand for labour in H change in the same proportion as does absorption there.

4

More light can be thrown on this process if the effects of changes in the money values are separated from those in the relative values. Suppose that initially the situation is as shown by the solid curves in Fig. 3. Both markets are in equilibrium. Excess of supply of exportables (both in value and in real terms) from country H is equal to the excess demand for them in the rest of the world W; and excess supply of importables from W is equal to the excess demand for them in H. Suppose, however, that the balance of payments is not in equilibrium. The value of exports from H, represented by the area $KMNL$ in the upper part of the diagram is not large enough to pay for the value of imports, represented by the area *kmnl* in the lower part of the diagram, and for capital transfers equal to the given balance on capital account. Money tends thus to flow from H to W and absorption, prices and wages tend to move downwards in the former and upwards in the latter.

Suppose now (for the purpose of analysis only) that for some quite arbitrary reason all money values in country H have fallen, all of them in the same proportion. We may call this first step in the analysis the value of money effect. It is what classical economists, brought up in the tradition of the quantity theory of money, would expect to happen in a closed economy. In accordance with some well known principles of economic theory, such uniform change in money values should have no effect on the quantities of goods supplied and demanded. Thus, if the prices of exportables and importables fell in country H from OP to OP', and from op to op', in the same proportion in the upper and in the lower part of the diagram, the supply and demand curves would have shifted at the same time so that the excess supply of exportables and excess demand for importables remained unchanged in real terms. The same would have to be true if in the rest of the world W all money values changed in the same proportion upwards. The curves of supply and demand on the left-hand side of the diagram would shift so that at the new level of prices the excess supply and the excess demand in real terms remained unchanged in W as well. If, therefore, those on the left-hand side of the diagram were equal to those on the right-hand side of it before the change in prices, they would have to remain so also after the change.

In Fig. 3 this new position is represented by the dotted curves. It is, however, not one of equilibrium. For the prices of the same goods are not the same on the two markets. Further adjustments must, therefore, take place for equilibrium of supply and demand to be finally attained.

5

Suppose now (again for the purpose of analysis only) that in the course of these further adjustments absorption remains unchanged. In the value of money effect, changes in the value of money only have been taken into account, not those in relative prices. Now changes in relative prices have to be superimposed on those in the general price level. They are brought about by adjustments in the flow of trade. The second step in the analysis may, therefore, be called the trade effect.

At the end of the first step, prices of both exportables and importables are lower in country H than in the rest of the world W. The tendency must be, therefore, for both of them to rise in the former and to fall in the latter. If the four systems of curves of supply and demand remained unchanged, equilibrium would establish itself at prices somewhere between P and P', and p and p'. In fact, however, the system of the curves would not remain unchanged. In the first place, the increase in both prices in country H, and the corresponding movement along both supply curves to the right, would mean that demand for labour in country H increases, wages increase, and both supply curves shift upwards. The opposite must be the case in the rest of the world W. In the second place, an increase in the price of importables in H has a substitution and an income effect on demand for exportables. According to whether the former or the latter is stronger, the curve of demand for exportables may thus shift to the left or to the right. Similarly the increase in the price of exportables must result in a shift, rightwards or leftwards, of the curve of demand for importables. In the rest of the world the two prices move downwards. Their substitution and income effects work thus in the opposite direction. The substitution effect tends to increase demand for the other good, and the income effect tends to reduce it.

It may be argued that in a country in which exports and imports play only a small part in its economy, these secondary shifts in the supply and demand curves are negligible. Equilibrium is than at some prices $P°$ and $p°$, not shown on the diagram, of

31

which supply is equal to demand in the upper and in the lower parts of the diagram, all of them determined by the dotted curves. If the increase in the value of exports, due to a greater quantity being sold by country H, and the decrease in the value of imports, due to a small quantity being bought, are sufficient to restore equilibrium of the balance of payments, no further movements of gold and foreign exchange are required, and no further adjustments in absorption, wages and prices need to take place. If, however, exports and imports play an important part in the economy, the trade effect cannot be neglected. As the demand curves are then pulled by the substitution effects and the income effects in opposite directions, shifts which result from them may still be dismissed as negligible. The supply curves, however, move quite definitely in the upward direction in the deficit country H (owing to an increase in wages there in relation to what they would be if there was no trade effect) and in the downwards direction in the rest of the world. Thus a part of the improvement in the balance of trade, which would have taken place if no shifts in the supply and demand curves occurred as a result of the trade effect, is now taken back. If a certain amount of outflow of gold and foreign exchange, and the corresponding shift of the supply and demand curves, was sufficient to restore equilibrium of the balance of payments through the value of money effect, it may not be sufficient if the trade effect is also taken into account.

6

More insight into the nature of the classical adjustments in the balance of trade can be gained if the aggregation of the variables is pushed a little further. The simplest model that an international-trade theorist has usually at the back of his mind is that in which (i) all goods produced in one country are treated as one aggregate, (ii) total output of those goods is given by the conditions of technique and of the available productive resources, and (iii) a part of that aggregate output is exported abroad in exchange for goods which in that country are not produced at all. The supply and demand relations for country H's exportables are then as in Fig. 4. The supply relation for exportables is represented by the vertical line SS at the point corresponding to full employment output; the demand relations for exportables are represented by DD in H and dd in W respectively; and the equilibrium price OP is determined by the condition $kO=KL$.

To allow for the possibility of disequilibrium in the balance of trade, aggregate income must be distinguished from absorption. For if the two were equal, the value of exports would have to be equal to the value of imports. That this is so can be easily shown on Fig. 4. Aggregate income in country H is represented there by the area of the rectangle $OPNL$. If absorption were equal to it, it would have to be also represented by that area. Spending on exportables, equal to the value of exportables sold on the home market is $OPMK$. The remaining part of $OPNL$, that is to say the area of the rectangle $KMNL$, would thus represent the value of exports as well as the value of imports. It would represent the former if it was interpreted as the difference between the value of all exportables produced ($OPNL$) and the values of those which have not been exported ($OPMK$): and it would represent the latter if it was interpreted as the difference between absorption ($OPNL$) and spending on exportables ($OPMK$). If absorption is different from aggregate income and is equal to $OPBA$, the value of exports is $KMNL$, the value of imports is $KMBA$, and the deficit of the balance of trade is $LNBA$.

7

Suppose now that, as was argued before, this deficit is not wholly covered by the surplus on capital account, and that as a result of a reduction in the quantity of money, wages, prices and absorption are reduced all of them in the same proportion. Let the dotted curves in Fig. 4 represent the new conditions of demand on the market for exportables. At the price OP' there is an excess demand for exportables equal to $k'k$ (because if all money values in country H decrease in the same

33

proportion, there is no change in demand for exportables there, and demand for them in W increases above the previous equilibrium level by $k'k$). As a result of the trade effect the equilibrium price of exportables tends to increase. If no further change in the position of the demand curves takes place, the price will ultimately settle down at some level $OP°$; and the deficit of the balance of trade will be reduced to $LN°B°A°$, $B°$ being on a rectangular hyperbolae passing through B' (because no change in absorption takes place in the course of the trade effect).

The curves of demand $D'D'$ and $d'd'$ might shift further as a result of similar adjustments on the market for importables (the details of which have here been omitted). It has been explained before that the direction of these shifts depends on the relative strength of the income effect and the substitution effect on demand for exportables of a change in the price of importables. It may be either way. If it happens that $D'D'$ shifts to the right, the equilibrium position moves downwards along the rectangular hyperbola passing through $B°$, and the ultimate improvement in the balance of trade is smaller. If $D'D'$ shifts to the left the improvement is greater. Similar considerations apply to the possible shifts of $d'd'$.

The nature of the process of adjustment in Fig. 4 is exactly the same as in Fig. 3. From the didactic point of view, however, the former has this advantage that it permits us to represent on the same diagram changes in the conditions of supply and demand on the one hand, and those in aggregate income and absorption on the other. The latter did not appear in Fig. 3 because there in addition to exportables and importables aggregate output and absorption also included domestic goods; and the existence of the latter was only allowed for in the analysis; it was not explicitly taken into account in the diagram. Adjustments in aggregate output and absorption play an even more important part in those aspects of the theory which are discussed in the remaining chapters of this book. This last section thus provides a useful link between the subject matter of the present chapter and that of the chapters to come.

8

In conclusion, a few words of explanation must be given about the significance of the supply-and-demand model which has been developed here. Changes in absorption (and in prices and wages) have been treated in it as a consequence of changes in the quantity of money. This was an essential aspect of the classical mechanism of international payments. In the hey-day of the gold standard, banks did in fact influence absorption (through a suitable credit policy) in the direction indicated by international gold movements, and the resulting shifts in the supply and demand relations must have had an equilibriating effect on the balance of payments. At present, however, this relation is not operative. It ceased to be operative after the First World War, when monetary policies of most countries became more and more concerned with problems of internal balance, of stable prices and a high level of employment, and less and less with those of external balance, of gold movements and stable exchange rates. This particular aspect of our supply-and-demand model is thus more in token of deference to a line of thought which had its great days in the past then in acknowledgement of a relation which is actually supposed to exist.

This, however, does not detract anything from the usefulness of the supply-and-demand model as a tool of analysis. Absorption, wages, and prices of domestic goods appear in it as parameters, and any changes in them may be allowed for when dealing with some actual situation; not only those which are the result of gold movements under the rules of the gold standard, but also those which the authorities may succeed in bringing about by all sorts of policy measures to achieve the objectives of internal balance. In some cases these may leave little scope for the distinction between the value-of-money effect and the trade effect on the position and form of the curves of supply and demand. There are, however, also cases, such for instance as that of devaluation, in the analysis of which we will find even this part of the tool useful.

IV

The Real Income Effect

THE analysis of the value of money and of the trade effects relies quite explicitly on two basic assumptions of classical economics. One of them is that the economy is always in the state of full employment, aggregate output being determined by the conditions of technique and the available productive resources. The other is that absorption in money terms and the price level are determined by the quantity of money. Thus a reduction in the quantity of money, due to an outflow of gold and foreign exchange reserves, leads to a fall in the money value of aggregate output, but it does not lead to any fall in the aggregate output itself.

The theory of international payments which has been developed under the influence of Keynes' *General Theory* differs from the classical theory on both those accounts. Real aggregate output is no longer regarded as given by the conditions of technique and the available productive resources but is determined by aggregate demand; and the price level is determined not by the quantity of money but by the level of wages and aggregate supply. In a Keynesian analysis of international trade the aggregate output must thus appear not as a datum but as a variable to be determined.

1

The first adjustment in our supply and demand model which has to be made to take these conditions into account is in the treatment of money wages. So far they have been regarded

36

as flexible both upwards and downwards, and influenced by changes in absorption in the same way as the general price level. In the Keynesian model wages are sticky, at least within the limits of those levels of income at which some unemployment still exists. The possibility of them becoming flexible upwards when the state of full employment is reached must not be excluded. It will, however, not be considered here. The analysis will be restricted to adjustments within the zone of some degree of unemployment, and within that zone money wages will be regarded as a datum.

This means that the supply curves of exportables, importables, and domestic goods, are data as well. For in the analysis which is the subject matter of this essay labour is supposed to be the only variable factor of production. As long, therefore, as the conditions of technique remain unchanged, wages are the only variable which could influence marginal costs. If they are constant, marginal costs and the supply curves must be constant as well.

What these curves actually are depends on what are the specific factors of production with which labour is combined and what are the conditions of technique. It would be quite legitimate to draw the supply curves as first downward sloping, owing to increasing returns to labour when very little of it is combined with a relatively large quantity of the specific factors, and then upward sloping as diminishing returns set in. In the modern conditions, however, there are reasons to believe that the marginal cost curves are fairly flat over the relevant range. They have the reversed L form, smoothed a little at the kink. To avoid unnecessary complications it may, therefore, be assumed that over the relevant range (before the kink is reached) all the supply curves are horizontal. Constant money wages mean then that prices are constant as well.

2

This simplifies matters in two respects. In the first place it allows us to abolish the distinction between real output and the money value of output. For as long as the price of an aggregate is constant, the money value of the latter may be accepted as a measure of its quantity. In a model of international trade in which exportables, importables, and domestic goods appear as variables, the money value of exports, imports, and of aggregate output may thus be identified with the volume of those exports, imports, and aggregate output.

Even this, however, allows for too much variety. For (and this is the second respect in which matters are simplified) constant prices allow us also to abolish the distinction between the aggregates. The problem of weighting different components of an aggregate does not then arise, because each component may be weighted by its constant price and all of them added together in money terms. And if the money value is identified with the volume of each particular aggregate, the volume of all the aggregates taken together may be identified with the money value of all of them. Two possibilities must then be considered. If the rate of exchange is also constant, no changes in money prices can occur, either within the country or in the rest of the world. All goods may then be treated as one. The model is in fact a one-aggregate model, and the distinction between exportables, importables, and domestic goods is in name only, to be taken into account or forgotten according to what the particular step in the argument requires. If the rate of exchange is not constant, money prices of home produced goods can be constant only if importables are not produced at home. For with the supply price of importables constant in terms of the currency of the rest of the world, a change in the rate of exchange is equivalent to a change in their price in terms of the currency of the importing country. In this case, therefore, two aggregates must be considered, exportables and domestic goods on one hand, and importables on the other. Specialisation must then be complete, importables not being produced in the importing country. For if this condition was not made, a constant supply price of importables in the importing country and a variable supply price of them abroad could be equal one to the other only by a fluke. In general, either the supply price abroad would have to be lower than that at home and the importables would not be produced in the importing country at all, or the home supply price would be lower and importables would not be importables but exportables.

Thus if the assumption of constant money wages and of horizontal supply curves for individual goods is accepted, the only model that needs be considered is one with a horizontal and constant supply curve of home-produced goods. Let it be PS' in Fig. 4. A decrease in absorption means then that the rectangle $OPBA$ becomes shorter, but its height remains the same. The aggregate output need not remain unchanged. The rectangle $OPNL$ may also become shorter, and the deficit of the balance of trade $LNBA$ may turn out to be not so much smaller as the reduction of absorption would indicate. This is in fact the main difference between the classical and the Keynesian analysis of the balance-of-payments adjustments. In the classical analysis the effect on the balance of trade of a reduction of absorption depends on how the price OP changes, the volume of output OL being constant. In the Keynesian analysis it depends on how the volume of output changes, the price being constant.[1]

3

Aggregate output in the Keynesian system is determined by aggregate demand and aggregate supply. In a simplified version of the model in which aggregate supply is supposed to be perfectly elastic at a given price (as in Fig. 4) the aggregate output is simply the aggregate quantity demanded at that price. The usual practice is to distinguish between three elements in the latter: an autonomous part, an income induced part, and that part which comes from abroad. The autonomous part and the demand from abroad are usually treated as given in absolute terms, and the induced part as a certain proportion of aggregate income. Thus
$$Y = E + I + hY$$
where Y represents income, E exports, I the autonomous part of

[1] For more advanced treatment of this subject see Vanek [35], Chapters 6–8.

aggregate demand, and h the coefficient which relates the induced part to the level of income. All of them refer to demand for home produced goods only. Demand for imports has no effect on Y.

The general criterion according to which aggregate demand is segregated into these three parts is not the purpose which the particular form of expenditure is supposed to serve but the factors on which its amount depends. Autonomous expenditure covers that part of investment, comsumption, and government expenditure on home produced goods, which is independent of the level of income. The income induced part is that which does depend on the level of income. In an elementary presentation of the Keynesian model the income induced part is usually identified with consumption, and the autonomous part with investment and government expenditure. From the point of view of the analysis offered in this book this is an unnecessary simplification. There are items in every consumer's and every firm's expenditure which are so basic that they may be regarded as virtually independent of the level of income; and there are forms of investment and of government expenditure which do depend on it. The analysis is not made either simpler or more elegant if we deny this fact. There is no need, therefore, to do it.

What, however, does make the analysis simple is (i) that goods and services that satisfy the three types of demand are treated as three aggregates, and (ii) that a linear relation is supposed to exist between the income induced part of aggregate demand and the level of income on which it depends. Quite enough has already been said in the first chapter of this book about the advantages and difficulties of aggregation. There is no need, therefore, to dwell on this subject again. Linearity of the relation for the income induced part is undoubtedly an arbitrary simplification introduced into the model in order to enable us to determine some of the effects of changes in the parameters by means of elementary algebra. At the cost of more labour, however, more complicated relations could be taken into account without any effect either on the general sense of the argument or on the conclusions.

4

Fig. 5 may be used to show how the variables introduced in the preceding section are determined. In the first (northeast) quadrant aggregate income Y in country H is measured along both axes; OA is absorption, OE exports, EI the autonomous part of aggregate demand for home produced goods, and the slope of the line IH is the coefficient h. Aggregate income is then equal to OY, and the difference YA represents the deficit of the balance of trade. If a 45° line is drawn through point S at which a horizontal line passing through E intersects the vertical line through Y, KY $(=OE)$ represents that part of the aggregate output OY which is exported, OK represents that part which is used at home, and KA is that part of absorption which is spent on imports. The picture is in fact very similar to that of Fig. 4. If a price scale were added along the vertical axis of Fig. 5, a horizontal supply curve could be inserted there, and the money values of absorption, income, exports, and of the balance of trade could be shown as areas of the same rectangles as in Fig. 4. As long, however, as prices are constant, no distinction need be made between money and real terms, and the supply and demand curves may be dispensed with. All the aggregates may be expressed in so small units, and the price per each of those units may be so low, that the band between the supply curve and the horizontal axis may reduce to a single line along the latter.

Absorption in this model is determined by the propensity to import function. It is assumed that a fixed proportion of absorption, the so called marginal propensity to import (to be denoted by m and shown by the slope of the line OU in the second quadrant of Fig. 5) is spent on imports. Equilibrium then requires that with absorption equal to OA demand for imports is $OM=KA$. If autonomous expenditure on home produced goods increased to EI', absorption and aggregate income would have to increase to OA' and OY' respectively. For it is only at that level that they would satisfy the conditions of equilibrium imposed by the fixed coefficients h and m, and by the given values of autonomous expenditure and of exports.

The analysis may easily be extended so as not to rely on any given value of exports. If both country H and the rest of the world W are put together, exports and imports become determined (simultaneously with aggregate income and absorption) by the autonomous parts of the aggregate demand in H and in W. To the relations on the right-hand side of Fig. 5 must be added those on the left-hand side corresponding to the rest of the world and plotted upside down as in Fig. 6. The condition of equilibrium which closes the system is that H's exports are equal to W's imports ($OE=Om$) and H's imports are equal to W's exports ($OM=Oe$).

Equilibrium implies also that YA on the right-hand side is equal to ya on the left-hand side of the diagram.

For if $OE = KY$ and $OM = KA$,
$$YA = OM - OE$$
And if $yk = Oe$ and $ak = Om$,
$$ya = Oe - Om$$

The result is not surprising. As has been explained before, the difference between absorption (OA) and aggregate income (OY) is always equal to the deficit of the balance of trade; and in a two-country model the deficit in H must always be equal to the surplus in W.

5

The effect on country H's economy of a change in the autonomous part of aggregate demand may be traced by shifting the IH and ih lines as the conditions of the change require. If, for instance, there is an increase in autonomous expenditure in country H, EI becomes greater. The impact effect of this change is that the line IH shifts upwards and Y moves to the right. Absorption increases as well and A moves to the right. This leads to an increase in imports OM and to a downward shift of ih in the rest of the world. The resulting adjustments on the left-hand side of the diagram react in turn on the position of IH on the right-hand side. And so the process of adjustment goes on until new equilibrium is established (shown by the dotted lines in Fig. 6). The ultimate increase in the aggregate income in county H is

$$YY' = (II'-EE')+EE'+h_hYY' \qquad \text{(i)}$$

and the increase in imports is

$$MM' = m_hAA' = AA'-YY'+EE' \qquad \text{(ii)}$$

In the rest of the world

$$y'y = MM'+h_wy'y \qquad \text{(iii)}$$

and $\qquad EE' = m_wa'a = a'a-y'y+MM' \qquad \text{(iv)}$

Hence, eliminating $y'y$ and $a'a$ from (iii) and (iv)

$$\frac{(1-m_w)}{m_w}EE' = \frac{h_w}{(1-h_w)}MM'. \qquad \text{(v)}$$

Substituting $AA'=(YY'-EE')/(1-m_h)$ from the right-hand side of (ii) into the left-hand side, and $MM'=m_h(YY'-EE')/(1-m_h)$ from there into (v) we obtain

$$EE' = \frac{m_wm_hh_w}{(1-m_w)(1-m_h)(1-h_w)+m_wm_hh_w}\ YY'$$

Thus from (i)

$$YY' = \frac{(1-m_w)(1-h_w)(1-m_h)+m_wh_wm_h}{k}(II'-EE')$$

$$EE' = \frac{m_wm_hh_w}{k}(II'-EE')$$

$$AA' = \frac{(1-m_w)(1-h_w)}{k}(II'-EE')$$

$$MM' = \frac{m_h(1-m_w)(1-h_w)}{k}(II'-EE')$$

and $(EE'-MM') = YY'-AA' = \dfrac{m_h[m_wh_w-(1-m_w)(1-h_w)]}{k}$

where $k = (1-m_w)\ (1-h_w)\ (1-m_h)\ (1-h_h) - m_w\ h_w\ m_h\ h_h$. It can then be shown that as long as $m+h<1$, $k>0$ and YY', EE', AA', and MM' are of the same sign as, and $(EE'-MM')$

of the opposite sign to that of $(II'-EE')$. An increase in autonomous spending leads to an expansion of income, of absorption, of exports and of imports, but to a deterioration of the balance of trade.

The formulae for the effect of $(II'-EE')$ on income and absorption in the rest of the world can be derived from (iii) and (iv). Thus

$$y'y = \frac{MM'}{1-h_w} = \frac{m_h(1-m_w)}{k} \,(II'-EE')$$

and

$$a'a = \frac{y'y}{1-m_w} - \frac{MM'}{1-m_w} = \frac{m_h h_w}{k} \,(II'-EE')$$

It can then be shown that $y'y-a'a=MM'-EE'$. Thus the solution satisfies the conditions that in the rest of the world also, the difference between the change in aggregate income and the change in absorption is equal to the improvement of the balance of trade.

6

The problem may also be approached in a slightly different way. A relation may be postulated between aggregate income and absorption. Suppose, for instance, that in Fig. 5 aggregate income is measured along the horizontal axis and absorption along the vertical axis. The relation between them may then be represented by the line ORC; the segment OR being equal to the autonomous part of absorption, and the slope of RC to what may be called the marginal propensity to absorb and denoted by c. If the aggregate income is OY, determined by the OIH relation, absorption is equal to OA, and the deficit of the balance of trade is YA. The diagram may then be extended along the lines already familiar. If OE represents exports, $KA=OM$ represent imports. The difference is only that now the proportion between absorption and imports needs not be constant. The relation between them is implied in the form of the lines ORC and OIH. The share of imports in the autonomous part of absorption is equal to $(1-EI/OR)$, and the share of imports in the income induced part is equal to $(1-h/c)$,

44

where h and c are the slopes of IH and RC respectively. If these two shares are equal one to the other, they must also be equal to OM/OA. The propensity to import relation might then be represented by a straight line passing through O and U. The slope of that line would be equal to $(1-h/c)$. If however the shares are not equal, no relation between imports and absorption can be shown in the southeast quadrant of the figure. The overall share of imports in absorption would then depend on the ratio of the autonomous to the induced parts of the latter. It could, therefore, be shown on the diagram only for some given and constant OR.

In the case of equal shares the solution can be obtained by using either the ORC curve or the OU curve. The former approach, however, applies also to those cases in which the shares are not equal. It is thus more general. It has further this advantage that it allows us to analyse the effect on the balance of trade of changes in exports and in the autonomous part of absorption in a more straightforward way than is possible with the other approach. An increase in exports means simply that the line IH shifts upwards, the point at which it intersects the 45° line moves towards Q, and the discrepancy YA which represents the deficit of the balance of trade declines. When the point of intersection passes beyond Q, the deficit turns into a surplus. An increase in autonomous absorption leads to both IH and RC shifting upwards. As, however, the increase in autonomous absorption is greater than the increase in autonomous spending on home produced goods (by that part of the former which is spent on imports), RC shifts upwards more than IH. This means that point Q shifts along the 45° line more than does the point at which IH intersects the 45° line, and the discrepancy YA becomes greater. Thus, as might have been expected, an increase in exports leads to an improvement, and an increase in autonomous expenditure to a deterioration of the balance of trade.

The diagram may be further extended by adding the rest of the world on the left-hand side. The conditions of equilibrium are then again that exports on one side are equal to imports on the other, and the effect on income, absorption, exports, and imports, of a change in autonomous absorption can be ascertained in more or less the same way as in the preceding section. The relevant formulae are

$$YY' = \frac{(c_w - h_w) + (1 - c_w)(1 - m)}{k'} RR'$$

$$EE' = (c_w - h_w)\frac{(1 - h_h) - (1 - c_h)(1 - m)}{k'} RR'$$

$$AA' = \frac{(c_w - h_w) + (1 - c_w)[(1 - h_h) + c_h(1 - m)]}{k'} RR'$$

$$MM' = (1 - h_w)\frac{(1 - h_h) - (1 - c_h)(1 - m)}{k'} RR'$$

$$(EE' - MM') = -(1 - c_w)\frac{(1 - h_h) - (1 - c_h)(1 - m)}{k'} RR'$$

$$yy' = \frac{(1 - h_h) - (1 - c_h)(1 - m)}{k'} RR'$$

and $\quad aa' = c_w\frac{(1 - h_h) - (1 - c_h)(1 - m)}{k'} RR'$

where $k' = (1 - c_h)(1 - h_w) - (1 - c_h)(1 - c_w) + (1 - c_w)(1 - h_h)$ and m is the share of imports in the autonomous part of absorption in country H. It can be shown by substituting $m = (1 - h/c)$ and $(II' - EE') = (h/c)RR'$ that if the share of imports is the same in the autonomous and in the induced parts of absorption, these formulae give the same changes in income, absorption, exports, and imports, as those which have been derived in Section 5.

7

Having done all this algebra the reader deserves an answer to the following two more general questions: (i) what are in fact the parameters of the relations in the Keynesian model of international payments; and (ii) what is the connection between the Keynesian approach to the theory of international trade and the supply-and-demand approach?

To answer the first part of the question let us consider once more the relations on which the Keynesian model actually depends. There are in fact two relations only that determine all the model's variables and are independent one of the other. One is that which relates aggregate absorption to national income; the other is that which relates the expenditure on imports to aggregate absorption. What is not spent on imports is spent on home produced goods. The latter relation determines thus also the expenditure on home produced goods as a function of aggregate absorption. And as aggregate absorption is a function of national income according to the first relation, the two relations together determine also the expenditure on home produced goods as a function of national income. This is what has been already explained in the first paragraph of the preceding section (using only different words and proceeding not from the relation between imports and absorption to that between income and home demand for home produced goods but the other way round, from spending on home produced goods as a function of income to imports as a function of absorption).

To decide what parameters are to be considered take first the relation between absorption and imports. It can be derived from that for D_m in (C) or in (D). According to (C) and (D) imports are a function of absorption and of the prices of all the aggregates in the model. The same must thus apply to the expenditure on imports. The prices must be, therefore, the parameters on which the form of the relation between absorption and imports depends. In a way the situation is just the opposite of what it was when (C) and (D) were used as demand relations. Absorption was then one of the parameters and the price of imports the argument of the function. Now the price of imports is a parameter and absorption the argument. All the other factors on which the form of the relation depends, not to be explicitly mentioned in the analysis, are supposed to be taken into account in the form of the function.

The relation between aggregate absorption and national income cannot be derived from any of the relations used in the supply-and-demand model. It represents an extension of the

47

model in the direction of making it more comprehensive by using an additional relation to transform absorption in (C) and (D) into a dependent variable. There is one new parameter in that relation: the autonomous part of absorption. Otherwise, the parameters are the same prices and wages which have been explicitly mentioned in the supply-and-demand model. The form of the relation is determined by all sorts of institutional, technical, and psychological factors. Prices and wages are the parameters because one may expect that any changes in them would affect aggregate absorption even if aggregate income remained unchanged. A fall in the prices of some imported raw materials might, for instance, stimulate investment in the industries in which those raw materials are used. It is difficult, however, to say anything definite about how in general changes in prices and wages would affect the relation.

8

A part of the answer to the second question, that about the connection between the two models, was already given in Section 3 above, where Fig. 5 was introduced as a development of Fig. 4, which in turn was developed from the supply and demand relations in Fig. 3. The preceding section went also some way towards clarifying the connection between the relations in the two models. This was, however, only a part of the answer, that about the connection between the techniques used. There still remains the part about the actual content of the analysis, about its subject matter.

In a box-of-tools economics the subject matter of the analysis is usually a model which fits approximately some class of situations and allows us to deal with each particular case in that class by making the necessary adjustments in the parameters. It is like an adjustable spanner which can be made to fit the size of any particular nut by a turn of the screw. The difficulty is only that in economics one class of situations cannot be so neatly separated from another as the fixing of a nut can be separated from the driving of a nail. The task of making an actual situation intelligible may be approached in various ways, and several tools may be needed to avail oneself of it. The supply-and-demand tool, for instance, may throw more light on one aspect of what actually takes place, and the real-income-effect tool on another.

To be more specific consider the following example. Suppose that an investment programme is going to be implemented in a country in which a large part of the installations required will have to be imported from abroad. How is this going to affect the flow of trade and international payments? One way of approaching the problem is to interpret the increase in investment as an increase in demand for imports, a rightward shift of the respective curve of demand, and to trace the effect of it by means of the supply-and-demand technique developed in Chapters II and III, allowing for such changes in the parameters of aggregate absorption, wages, and prices of domestic goods as in this particular situation may be expected to occur. The other way is to interpret the increase in investment as an increase in autonomous spending and to trace the effect of it on trade by means of the real-income technique developed in Chapter IV, allowing for all the possible changes in the parameters of wages and prices.

This is how the contents of the two lines of analysis are related one to the other. If the nature of the connection between them is well apprehended and the tools which they offer are used together, one line may help to understand better what happens to the parameters of the other line, and more insight can be gained in this way into the actual working of the system as a whole.

V

The Rate of Exchange

THE technique developed in the preceding chapters may now be used to answer the first of the two questions set at the beginning. What factors determine the rate of exchange? As this rate is the price of foreign exchange, determined on the market for foreign exchange, the question is in fact about the factors which determine the supply and demand for it. They are the parameters on which the solution of the supply and demand equation ultimately depends. It has been explained already that the number of the factors may be quite large and that they may be related one to another in various ways. The analysis offered in this chapter attempts, therefore, to throw some light on the problem by removing some of those parameters from the equation; either by means of the *ceteris paribus* clause, or by means of additional relations introduced into the model to transform the parameters into variables and eliminate them from the system altogether.

1

Two points have to be made at the beginning. One concerns the part which capital and other non-trade transactions may play in the determination of the rate of exchange. The other concerns the part played by public policy and all sorts of institutional arrangements.

With respect to the first point it has been already explained that one of the limitations of the theory expounded in this essay is that it does not allow for non-trade transactions to be treated as variables. They can be allowed for in it, but only as data.

Hence the supply of foreign exchange resulting from capital imports, gifts, etc., and the demand for foreign exchange resulting from capital exports, etc. must be treated as given parameters of the supply-and-demand equation. Equilibrium of supply and demand for foreign exchange does not imply that the balance of trade is in equilibrium. But (subject to the reservation made in the next paragraph) it does imply that the balance of trade shows a given deficit or surplus.

With respect to the second point, it must be emphasised that if the authorities have sufficient reserves of home currency and of foreign exchange, the rate of exchange may be maintained by them at any level, by making home currency and foreign exchange available in unlimited quantities at that rate. The gold standard is an example of institutional arrangements devised for the purpose of stabilizing the rate of exchange permanently at a chosen level. In modern conditions the rate of exchange is usually 'pegged' in a much less permanent sense by the government's decision to intervene whenever there is a tendency for it to deviate from that level. Permanent stabilisation requires equilibrium of the balance of payments in the long run. For if the reserves become exhausted, the intervention must cease. It may be argued, however, that equilibrium of the balance of payments can be achieved through changes in the value of money or in real national income along the lines indicated in Chapters III and IV. Even, therefore, in the long run the rate of exchange might be regarded as determined quite arbitrarily by the authorities.

This is, of course, not the kind of determination that is the subject matter of the present chapter. It is assumed here that the authorities leave the foreign exchange market to find its equilibrium through such adjustments in the rate of exchange as the parameters of the supply-and-demand equation require. This does not necessarily mean that the authorities do not intervene at all. They may be actively engaged in smoothing out day to day fluctuations in the exchange, due to accidental factors. The assumption means, however, that with those accidental factors eliminated, the smoothed out rate of exchange is determined by

51

the conditions of supply and demand, and not the conditions of supply and demand by the rate of exchange. The authorities influence only the process through which the rate of exchange reaches its equilibrium level. They do not influence the level itself.

2

The simplest model that may be devised to analyse the working of the supply and demand mechanism for foreign exchange is that of given and constant supply and demand curves.[1] The analysis is then similar to that of Chapter III. The difference is only that the rate of exchange is now treated not as a parameter but as a variable to be determined. Thus the scale along the vertical axis in Fig. 3 may now change in response to pressures of supply and demand for foreign currency, and as a result of this the curves on the right-hand side of the diagram may shift upwards or downwards in relation to those on the left-hand side. As long as the factors determining the form of the curves are treated as data, the curves shift proportionately, each point on each curve by the same proportion of its distance from the horizontal axis. The adjustments in trade may then be due solely to what was described previously as the value-of-money effect. If originally the foreign exchange market is not in equilibrium because the value of exports is too small in relation to that of imports, the rate of exchange of country H's currency must fall, the curves on the right-hand side of the diagram shift downwards in relation to those on the left-hand side, the prices of exportables and of importables fall in terms of foreign currency and increase in terms of home currency, the quantity of exports from country H increases and the quantity of imports decreases. The value of imports into country H must then fall, and if the value of exports increases (or at least falls less than the value of imports), the market for foreign exchange moves towards a position of equilibrium. The rate of exchange finds its equilibrium level when the shifts of the curves have gone so far that

[1] See the analysis offered by Joan Robinson [28] and Machlup [14]. A textbook exposition of the points discussed in this Chapter may be found in Kindleberger [8] Chapters 9, 10 and 11.

the difference between the value of exports and the value of imports is just sufficient to cover the deficit or to offset the surplus of the autonomous part of the balance of payments.

It has been often maintained that the equilibrium rate of exchange is determined by the purchasing power of the respective currencies. This is the so called Purchasing Power Parity Theory.[1] It is clear from what has been said in this section that if specialisation is incomplete and both exportables and importables are produced in country H and in the rest of the world W, one of the conditions of equilibrium is that (neglecting transport and other costs of moving goods from country to country) prices of exportables and of importables are the same in H and in W (if expressed in the same currency). This, however, does not mean that the rate of exchange is determined by the purchasing power parity of the currencies. For the condition of equal prices may be satisfied at various rates of exchange according to what are the other items in the balance of payments. The power of the respective currencies to purchase exportables and importables is thus determined simultaneously with the rate of exchange by the conditions of supply and demand for goods and services, including capital and all other autonomous items in the balance of payments. Furthermore, the power of the currencies to purchase exportables and importables must not be identified with their general purchasing power. There are also domestic goods in H and in W, whose prices need not be the same when the market for foreign exchange is in equilibrium. It is, therefore, only in the sense of some very loose and general rule of thumb that the Purchasing Power Parity Theory may be accepted as valid. If the respective currencies can buy more or less the same baskets of goods, there is a fair chance that the discrepancies between supply and demand for particular goods (distributed at random over all of them) would cancel out, and the balance of trade would be in equilibrium.

---

[1] For a more detached discussion see Haberler [4] pp. 32 ff.

3

The conditions for the pressures of supply and demand for foreign currency pushing the rate of exchange towards an equilibrium level are usually given in terms of the elasticities of supply and demand for exports and imports. In the upper part of Fig. 7 DS represents supply of exportables for export from country H, and SD represents demand for imports of those exportables into the rest of the world W. In the lower part of the figure the curves ds and sd represent demand for imports in country H and supply of exports from the rest of the world. The nature of the relations shown by these curves has been already explained in the second section of Chapter II. If now, as a result of a disequilibrium of supply and demand for foreign exchange, the rate of exchange moved against country H, the supply curve of exports DS and the demand curve for imports ds shift downwards in proportion to the change in the rate of exchange (equal to $EE'/ET=mm'/mt$ for instance). It is then clear that if the elasticity of demand for exports (the elasticity of the SD curve) is equal to unity, the value of exports in terms of foreign currency is unchanged. If the elasticity is greater than unity, the value of exports increases. By turning the supply curve $D'S'$ around point E' it can be also shown that in this latter case the increase in the value of exports is greater the more elastic is supply. Similarly, by changing the slope of the $d's'$ curve around point m' it can be shown that the value of imports in terms of foreign currency falls more the more elastic is the demand for imports. And by turning the supply curve sd around point m it can be shown that if the elasticity of $d's'$ is greater than unity, more elastic sd means that the reduction in the value of imports is greater; and if the elasticity of demand for the former is less than unity, more elastic supply means that the reduction in the value of imports is smaller.

The overall effect on the balance of trade is all these tendencies added up together. The relevant formula may be derived as follows. The change in the value of exports in terms of foreign currency is equal to

$$OP' \cdot TT' - PP' \cdot OT = \left(\frac{TT'}{PP'} \cdot \frac{OP'}{OT} - 1 \right) \frac{PP'}{OP} \cdot OP \cdot OT$$

The first term in the bracket represents the elasticity of demand for exports (to be denoted by ε_e); and the last term on the right-hand side is the total value of exports. The ratio PP'/OP' can be eliminated by using the well known proposition about the burden of an indirect tax. The proposition says that

$$\frac{PP'}{EE' - PP'} = \frac{\sigma_e}{\varepsilon_e}$$

where σ_e and ε_e are the elasticities of supply and demand respectively. Collecting terms and bearing in mind that EE'/OP (to be denoted by $\Delta r/r$) is the rate of change of the rate of exchange, the above may be reduced to

$$\frac{PP'}{Op} = \frac{\sigma_e}{\varepsilon_e + \sigma_e} \cdot \frac{\Delta r}{r}$$

and the formula for the change in the value of exports becomes

$$\frac{\sigma_e(\varepsilon_e - 1)}{\varepsilon_e + \sigma_e} \cdot \frac{\Delta r}{r}$$

Similarly the change in the value of imports is

$$-mm' \cdot ot - m't \cdot tt' + (mm' - pp')ot' = -\left[1 + \frac{\sigma_m(\varepsilon_m - 1)}{\varepsilon_m + \sigma_m} \right] \frac{\Delta r}{r} \cdot op \cdot ot$$

(the difference between $op \cdot ot / op' \cdot ot'$ and unity being neglected). The change in the balance of trade is then the difference between the change in the value of exports and that in the value of imports. Expressed as a percentage of the value of imports it is equal to[1]

$$\frac{\Delta B}{M} = \left[b \frac{\sigma_e(\varepsilon_e - 1)}{\varepsilon_e + \sigma_e} + \frac{\sigma_m(\varepsilon_m - 1)}{\varepsilon_m + \sigma_m} + 1 \right] \frac{\Delta r}{r}$$

[1] The formula differs from that derived by Joan Robinson [28] because it refers to the balance of trade in terms of foreign currency whereas Joan Robinson's formula refers to the balance of trade in terms of home currency. It agrees with that given by Kindleberger [8] p. 658.

This general result is often simplified by assuming that the elasticity of supply approaches infinity and trade is initially balanced. The formula reduces then to

$$\frac{\Delta B}{M} = (\varepsilon_e + \varepsilon_m - 1)\frac{\Delta r}{r} \qquad (E)$$

Thus if in this special case the sum of the elasticities of demand is greater than unity, a fall in the rate of exchange due to a deficit of the balance of payments leads to an improvement of the balance of trade and to a movement towards a new position of equilibrium. If the sum of the two elasticities is less than unity, a fall in the rate of exchange leads to a deterioration of the balance of trade and to a movement further and further away from the position of equilibrium. In the general case the numerical values of the elasticities of demand are not the only factors determining the direction in which the balance of trade will move. The elasticities of supply and the balance of trade ratio must also be taken into account.

4

The formal parts of the supply and demand theory of the rate of exchange are quite simple. As soon as the supply and demand relations for exports and imports are accepted as data, the adjustments in the rate of exchange and in supply and demand for foreign exchange can be derived from them by simple algebra. The interpretation, however, of these relations invites a critical comment.

In the first place it must be emphasised that particular equilibrium techniques have been transplanted here from a field of single commodities to that of whole aggregates, and that in this latter case the use of the *ceteris paribus* clause is not as legitimate as in the former. In the present essay the factors affecting the form of the supply and demand relations have been subsumed under four headings: absorption, wages, prices of domestic goods, and prices of importables or exportables according to whether the supply and demand relations are those for the latter or for the former. If, therefore, the clause *ceteris paribus* is applied to all supply and demand relations, all these factors must be regarded as independent of what happens on the markets for exportables and importables, and for foreign exchange. As far as the amount of absorption and the level of wages is concerned, it may be argued that if only a small proportion of income is derived from the production of goods for export and only a small part of absorption is spent on imports, the amount of absorption and the level of wages (and in consequence the prices of domestic goods) are determined by factors and policy considerations which are influenced to a negligible extent only by the conditions of foreign trade. From the point of view of the theory of the latter, they may therefore be accepted as data. Changes in prices of exportables and importables cannot be assumed away by means of the *ceteris paribus* clause, for they are an important element in the whole process of adjustment. What is required in this case is rather that the existence of the cross relations between them and the conditions of supply and demand can be neglected.

If the actual conditions are such that neither of these assumptions applies (that is to say if the policies determining absorption, wages, and prices of domestic goods are influenced by what happens on the markets for exportables and importables, and the cross effects between the latter are not negligible), the supply and demand relations may still be treated as data if they are redefined so that they take into account the possible changes in the parameters on which their *ceteris paribus* form depends. Take, for instance, the case of the reduction of the general formula for the effect on the balance of trade of an exchange rate adjustment to the form expressed in (E) by means of the assumption that the elasticities of supply of exports approach infinity. The assumption may be interpreted in two ways. One of them is that a small proportion only of the total output of exportables is actually exported, and that the possible adjustments in the volume of exports are only marginal in relation to the total output of exportables. Practically no change in the supply price can, therefore, be associated with these adjustments

57

even if the respective industries are subject to diminishing returns and wages are constant; and practically no changes in wages may be expected to result from them. This is a particular-equilibrium interpretation corresponding to the conditions described in the preceding paragraph. The elasticities which appear in (E) are then also particular-equilibrium elasticities, subject to the *ceteris paribus* clause with respect to the total amount of absorption. For no change in the latter may be expected to result from the marginal adjustments in the output of exportables either.

It is possible, however, to give the assumption of perfectly elastic supply curves a different, 'total' interpretation. It may be argued that if all home-produced goods form one aggregate, the condition of internal balance of the country may be identified with that of the price of that aggregate being kept constant. Whatever the demand for these goods for export and whatever the amount of exports actually supplied, the supply price always remains the same. Thus again the supply of exports is perfectly elastic. In this case, however, the assumption of marginality of changes in exports in relation to the total output of exportables is no longer needed. For the objective of a constant price level of home-produced goods can always be achieved by a suitable adjustment of absorption. What is needed is a reinterpretation of the elasticities of demand which appear in (E). They cease to be 'partial' elasticities subject to the *ceteris paribus* clause with respect to absorption, and become 'total' elasticities summarising the form of the demand relations in which the necessary changes in absorption are already taken into account.[1] This point must be emphasised. If the *ceteris paribus* conditions of particular equilibrium are not satisfied, the given supply and demand conditions from which formula (E) derives are not those of the conventional curves of supply and demand. They imply such reactions of the whole economic system as are called forth by the requirements of internal balance (or by such other additional relations between absorption, output, wages, and prices

[1] The distinction between 'partial' and 'total' elasticities of demand has been introduced by Pearce [25] and is elaborated further in Section 8 of Chapter VI.

of home-produced goods, as we may wish to introduce into the model). The simplicity of the partial equilibrium approach is then bought at a very high price. For if the relations defined by these requirements are not explicitly taken into account but only supposed to be covered by the form of the supply and demand relations, then instead of elucidating the part played in the process of adjustment by all the factors which are regarded as relevant, the analysis only conceals some of those factors and misrepresents the part played by the others.

5

Changes in absorption may be brought explicitly into the model by using the technique developed in the last section of Chapter IV. The deficit of the balance of trade in terms of home-produced goods is determined there as the difference between aggregate absorption and aggregate income. The change in the balance of trade, brought about by an adjustment in the rate of exchange, must thus be equal to the difference between the changes in absorption and income. The analysis of the factors on which the result depends was given for the first time by Alexander.[1] The technique developed in this essay may be applied to elucidate the general sense of it.

A change in exports may be taken as the starting point. A downward adjustment in the rate of exchange means that the demand curve for exports shifts upwards, and the volume of exports increases. This means that point E in Fig. 5 shifts upwards, and so does the line IH. If all the parameters of the relations shown in the figure remain unchanged, the point at which IH intersects the 45° line moves upwards towards Q and the deficit of the balance of trade becomes smaller. The change in absorption, induced by the change in income, is then $c\Delta Y$, the change in income is $\Delta Y = \Delta E/(1-h)$, and the change in the balance of trade is $\Delta Y - c\Delta Y = [(1-c)/(1-h)]\Delta E$. As absorption

[1] See also Machlup [13]. It must be emphasised that Alexander's analysis (as well as that which is given in this and the next two sections of this essay) refers to the balance of trade *in terms of home produced goods*.

increases, imports increase as well, and this affects income and absorption abroad. The demand curve for exports from country H shifts therefore still further up, and so does point E in Fig. 5. The ultimate increase in exports ΔE and the ultimate increase in income ΔY will thus be greater than those which correspond to the initial shift of the point E (due to the impact effect of the adjustment in the rate of exchange).

It thus appears that as long as the marginal propensity to absorb c is less than unity, a downward adjustment in the rate of exchange should have a favourable effect on the balance of trade. The condition, however, is that all the parameters of all the relations in Fig. 5 remain unchanged. In fact changes in them are very likely to take place, due to quite a number of causes. The adjustment in the rate of exchange may, for instance, result in a redistribution of income, which in turn may affect the marginal propensity to absorb c and the marginal propensity to spend on home-produced goods h. Or a change in the quantity of money, due to an improvement of the balance of payments, may affect the rate of interest which in turn may influence both the autonomous and the induced parts of absorption. Full discussion of these factors is outside the scope of the present volume. They may be assumed away by means of the *ceteris paribus* clause or by aggregation. What, however, has to be considered more carefully even in the limited context of an aggregative model is the possibility of the relations on which the result depends being affected by changes in prices and in wages which accompany the adjustment of the rate of exchange.

6

Consider the case in which exportables are the only goods produced in country H and money wages are constant. The supply curve of home-produced goods is horizontal over the whole relevant range. In other words full employment has not been reached yet, and is supposed not to be reached as a result of the contemplated adjustments in the rate of exchange. The price of exportables is then also constant, and it does not matter whether exports are expressed in quantity or in money. In the case of the other variables the relation between money value and real value in terms of home-produced goods is more complicated. For, as a result of an increase in demand for imports in country H and of an upward shift of the supply curve of them in the rest of the world (due to the downward adjustment in the rate of exchange), the price of imports in terms of country H's currency may be expected to increase. This means that the same amount of absorption in terms of home-produced goods now represents a smaller basket of goods bought (if importables are included in it). If, therefore, the autonomous part of absorption represents a certain basket of both types of goods, its amount in terms of home-produced goods may be expected to increase, and point R in Fig. 5 may be expected to move upwards.

An increase in the price of imports in terms of home currency (and therefore in terms of home-produced goods) means also that a given increase in income in terms of home-produced goods represents a smaller income in 'real' terms. Similarly a given amount of induced absorption in terms of home-produced goods represents a smaller amount in 'real' terms. If then the RC relation is in 'real' terms, and 'real' income and 'real' induced absorption are not affected by the change in the price of imports both of them exactly in the same proportion, the slope of RC is bound to change.

It is further possible that changes in relative prices may affect the position and the slope of the line IH. For, if imports become more expensive than home-produced goods, there is likely to be a tendency for the latter to be substituted for the former. Thus a different proportion (greater or smaller according to what is the respective elasticity of substitution) of any given autonomous absorption will be spent on home-produced goods, and the line IH will shift upwards or downwards. Similarly, a different proportion of the induced part of absorption may then be spent on home-produced goods, and the slope of IH may change as well.

It is very difficult to say what might be the net effect of all these shifts. As they pull in different directions, the net effect is not likely to be large, and its direction is uncertain. One may be tempted, therefore, to neglect them altogether. It is, however, well to bear in mind that some shifts in the relevant relations are bound to occur.

7

At the other extreme, when the economy of country H is in the state of full employment and the supply curve of home-produced goods is vertical, a downward adjustment of the rate of exchange cannot result in any increase in income in terms of those goods. The latter is determined by the intersection of a vertical line drawn through the point of full employment with the 45° line. It is, therefore, the form of the OIH line that would have to adjust itself to the given level of Y and not the other way round. If absorption increased in money terms, either the prices would have to increase as well, so that 'real' absorption would remain unchanged; or a smaller proportion of the increased absorption would have to be spent on home-produced goods, so that the point of intersection of IH with the 45° line would remain where it was. Thus in this case an increase in the volume of exports, brought about by a downward adjustment in the rate of exchange, would have to be accompanied either by a reduction in the autonomous expenditure on home-produced goods or by a reduction of the coefficient h (or by both). The only effect, therefore, that the adjustment in the rate of exchange could have on the balance of trade in terms of home-produced goods would be through shifts in the relation ORC.

What these shifts would be depends again on how relative prices change and on the possibility of substituting home-produced goods for imports. All the remarks made at the end of the preceding section apply to this case as well: with this reservation only that now the price of exports may also be expected to change, and that nothing definite can therefore be said about the direction in which the relative prices would move. The model developed by Alexander is thus not of much help if full employment prevails. It does not say how the *ORC* relation would change. And if *ORC* does not change, the adjustment in the rate of exchange cannot have any effect on the balance of trade in terms of home-produced goods.

8

In conclusion, a few remarks may be added about the relation between the supply-and-demand approach and the absorption approach, following the lines which should be familiar by now. The difference between the two approaches is that they are using different models. The supply-and-demand approach is using a model in which prices of importables and exportables are variables, and absorption in money terms is a parameter; and the absorption approach uses a model in which the prices are parameters, and absorption is a variable. The relation between them is thus just that between the Keynesian and the supply-and-demand models. The models complement each other, one taking up the analysis where the other leaves it. The absorption model helps us to understand what happens to some of the parameters of the supply-and-demand model; and *vice versa*, the latter helps us to make allowances for possible changes in the parameters of the former.

The point is particularly important if the purpose of the analysis is to make intelligible any of the actual events in more recent years. The conditions of most of the countries in the postwar world have been neither those of full-employment income determined solely by technical relations and available productive resources, nor those of unemployment and perfectly elastic aggregate supply. Neither the supply-and-demand model nor the absorption model approximates thus very closely the actual state of affairs. Changes in the rate of exchange must be expected to lead in these conditions to changes in prices as well as to those in real aggregate income and absorption. Both models, therefore, have to be used to bring into focus all the connections between the relevant variables. In the form in which they have been developed in this chapter they cannot be combined into one more comprehensive model, capable of a straightforward answer to any question that may be put to it. They supplement, however, each other as tools of analysis, which have to be used with skill and understanding of the problem in hand to be effective.

VI

The Terms of Trade

LITTLE so far has been said about the terms of trade. Changes in them have been implied in nearly every form of adjustment considered because adjustments in money prices imply usually adjustments in their ratios. From many a point of view, however, adjustments in the terms of trade may be regarded as more important than those in the absolute level of prices. They are an indication of how the gains from trade are divided between the countries concerned. It is necessary, therefore, at least at this late stage, to take them more explicitly into account, and to subject the possible adjustments in them to a more careful analysis than has been made so far.

1

Identities (A) and (B) may be used again to explain in more precise terms the problem with which this chapter will be concerned. Identity (A)

$$\frac{T}{r} \equiv \frac{p}{P}$$

derives from the definition of the terms of trade and relates them to money prices p, P and to the rate of exchange r. Identity (B)

$$Tb \equiv \frac{E}{M}$$

relates the terms of trade to the balance of trade ratio b and to the volume of exports E, M. All these are variables to be determined.

65

The supply and demand technique has been used in the preceding chapters to determine the variables on the right-hand side of the equations. Four supply and demand relations, represented by the supply and demand curves in country H and in the rest of the world W (and given in terms of the parameters on which their form depends) are sufficient to determine the two prices p, P and the two quantities E, M. The number of the variables is thus reduced to three: T, r and b which appear on the left-hand side of (A) and (B). Even then, however, there is one of them too many. For there are only two identities to determine them. Some additional condition must thus be introduced into the model to have a determinate solution.

In the preceding chapters two possibilities have been considered. One was that the rate of exchange r was supposed to be given and constant. Thus for any pair of prices determined by the conditions of supply and demand the terms of trade T were determined by identity (A); and for any given pair of quantities determined by the same conditions of supply and demand the balance of trade ratio b was determined by identity (B). Then the analysis either stopped at that, or it allowed for a disequilibrium in the balance of payments affecting in turn the supply and demand conditions through changes in absorption, until b reached some equilibrium value consistent with the other items in the balance of payments. In this latter case b was thus not a variable either. It was given as a residue of those other items in the balance of payments. The system, however, was not overdetermined because absorption as a factor determining the supply and demand conditions assumed the role of a variable. The second possibility was that the rate of exchange was treated as a variable and affected the conditions of supply and demand so as to give b the required value without any (or with only some incidental) changes in absorption.

In the discussion of both these cases the focus was on the rate of exchange and on the balance of trade. That in the course of the process of adjustment some changes in the terms of trade had to take place was well understood. Not much attention, however, was paid to them and no attempt was made to determine the direction in which they would go. This is, therefore, what has to be done now. In the remaining sections of this chapter the technique developed before will be used to elucidate the factors which determine the direction of possible adjustments in the terms of trade.

2

Not much can be said about these adjustments on the ground of the relation expressed in (A). In Fig. 3 the money prices of exportables and importables are determined by the condition that subject to the given supply and demand relations both markets are in equilibrium. The ratio of the two prices is the terms of trade determined by the same set of relations. The adjustments in it may be due to two tendencies. A disequilibrium of the balance of payments may result in an adjustment in the rate of exchange and in a shift of the whole supply and demand system on one side of the diagram relative to that on the other. Alternatively, a change in absorption may take place, either as a result of the disequilibrium of the balance of payments and the corresponding gold and foreign exchange movements, or brought about deliberately by the authorities; and the supply and demand relations may shift in response to that change.

If in the case of exchange rate adjustments the shifts of the supply and demand curves due to cross effects of changes in prices and to changes in absorption and in wage rates are neglected, an adjustment of the rate of exchange must result in a movement of the prices of exportables and importables, both of them in the same direction. The changes in the terms of trade which would emerge from these movements may thus be a deterioration as well as an improvement. The same is true if there is a change in absorption and wages are flexible. The value-of-money effect of such change is identical with that of an adjustment in the rate of exchange, and the same conclusions apply.

Using Fig. 7 and the first steps of the proof which led to the result expressed in (E) it can be shown that the proportional change in the price of exportables in terms of foreign currency is

$$\frac{PP'}{OP} = \frac{\sigma_e}{\varepsilon_e + \sigma_e} \cdot \frac{\Delta r}{r}$$

Similarly (remembering, however, that in the bottom part of the diagram the positions of the supply and demand curves are reversed) it can be shown that the proportional change in the price of importables is

$$\frac{pp'}{op} = \frac{\varepsilon_m}{\varepsilon_m + \sigma_m} \cdot \frac{\Delta r}{r}$$

The proportional change in the terms of trade is then the difference between the latter and the former, i.e.

$$\frac{\Delta T}{T} = \frac{\varepsilon_e \varepsilon_m - \sigma_e \sigma_m}{(\varepsilon_e + \sigma_e)(\varepsilon_m + \sigma_m)} \cdot \frac{\Delta r}{r}$$

Thus the terms of trade move in the same or in the opposite direction to that of the rate of exchange according to whether the product of the two elasticities of demand is greater or smaller than the product of the two elasticities of supply.[1]

3

The traditional approach to the problem is through identity (B). It is argued that a disequilibrium of the balance of payments may appear over short periods only. In the long run the balance of payments must be in equilibrium because it is impossible either to accumulate or to decumulate foreign exchange indefinitely. The ratio b is thus given, determined by the autonomous items in the balance of payments and assumed to be equal to unity to make the analysis simple; and the number of variables is reduced to three T, E and M. To determine them two additional relations are introduced in the form of the so called reciprocal demand functions, one for the country H and one for the rest of the world W. They solve for the quantities E and M, and the terms of trade are then obtained from (B).

The concept of reciprocal demand was introduced into the

[1] This condition is derived by Vanek in [35] p. 79.

theory of international trade by John Stuart Mill[1] to fill a gap in Ricardo's theory of comparative cost. The latter did not explain at what terms exports exchange for imports. Cost ratios set only the limits within which the terms of trade must fall. Their actual value has to be determined by the conditions of demand. The condition that exports exchange for imports implies that the balance of trade is in equilibrium. Hence the notion of reciprocal demand, of demand for imports in exchange for exports. The analysis was subsequently refined by Marshall, and in more recent times by Lerner, Leontief, Scitovsky, Meade, and others.[2]

The general sense of it is that to each possible ratio of exchange, that is to say to each possible terms of trade, correspond certain quantities of exports and of imports, which satisfy the condition that the respective country is in equilibrium both internally and externally. The former means that all markets, including that for labour, are in equilibrium at full employment; the latter means that the balance of trade (identified in this simple model with the balance of payments) in in equilibrium. These quantities of exports and imports may be plotted on a diagram, exports along the horizontal axis and imports along the vertical axis, and a curve may be drawn to show the relation between them and the given terms of trade, e.g. OQ in Fig. 8. To the terms of trade given by the slope of the line OT, for instance, correspond exports equal to OE and imports equal to OM. The curve is usually called an offer curve.

A similar curve may be drawn for the rest of the world. In Fig. 8 it is drawn with axes reversed and is represented by Oq. Point E at which the two curves intersect represents equilibrium of supply and demand for both exports and imports. For OM is there both offered by the rest of the world W and demanded by country H; and OE is both offered by country H and demanded by the rest of the world W. The slope of OT represents the equilibrium terms of trade.

[1] [20] Book 3, Chapter XIII. See also Haberler [4] Chapter XI, and Kindleberger [8] Chapter 6.

[2] Scitovsky [33], Marshall [15], Lerner [11], Leontief [9], Meade [16] and [17].

4

Offer curves OQ and Oq imply such adjustments in supply and demand for exportables and importables as are necessary to keep the balance of trade in equilibrium. In principle they could, therefore, be derived from such movements along and shifts of the supply and demand curves for exportables and importables as correspond to the conditions of balanced trade. To show what adjustments the offer curves actually embody, it may be useful to trace some of these movements and shifts. Any pair of supply and demand curves for exportables and importables of country H may be taken as the starting point. To result in a point on an offer curve the prices must be so chosen that the balance of trade is in equilibrium. If, for instance, OP and op in Fig. 3 satisfy this condition, that is to say if $KMNL=kmnl$, the quantity of exports to be plotted along the horizontal axis of an offer curve diagram is KL, the quantity of imports to be plotted along the vertical axis is kl and the slope of the line of the terms of trade is $kl/KL=OP/op$ (because $KL.OP=kl.op$).

The rest of the offer curve may then be traced by taking some arbitrary changes in the world market prices. It may, for instance, be assumed that demand for imports in country H is elastic, and that owing to some changes in the conditions of supply and demand abroad the price of exportables OP increases and the price of importables op decreases so that there is no change in the balance of trade. The value of exports increases exactly as much as does the value of imports. This is equivalent to a movement along the offer curve to a point corresponding to more favourable terms of trade and to a greater volume of both imports and exports. As, however, the price of exports increases and the prices of imports decreases, the quantity of exports must increase less than in proportion to the quantity of imports, and the offer curve has the familiar upward bend. If at some low level of op the demand curve for imports becomes inelastic, no further increase in the price of exportables is possible. For the resulting increase in the value of exports could not

70

then be matched by an increase in the value of imports. The offer curve could then be traced further only by both prices being reduced, and it would bend to the left. For from now onwards, further increases in the quantity of imports would have to be accompanied by reductions in the quantity of exports. The terms of trade would continue to improve.

5

The assumption that changes in money prices are exactly such as are necessary to maintain the balance of trade in equilibrium under *ceteris paribus* conditions of supply and demand is, of course, quite arbitrary. So are the *ceteris paribus* conditions themselves. In fact adjustments in the position of the supply and demand curves are bound to occur both as a result of cross effects of whatever changes in prices do actually take place, and as a result of adjustment in the rate of exchange, in absorption, and in the level of wages, through which the balance of trade is kept in equilibrium. The shifts in the position of the curves of supply and demand must affect the form of the offer curves. It is, however, usually admitted that in spite of these shifts an offer curve is most likely to have an upward bending form as in Fig. 8.

One of the reasons for this is a close correspondence between an offer curve of a country and a price-consumption curve of an individual. Both may be traced by joining together the points of tangency of successive indifference curves with the corresponding price lines. The concept of a unique system of indifference curves of a whole country is subject to many reservations.[1] If, however, a system of this kind exists, it must have a form similar to that of an individual consumer. The indifference curves of country H, drawn with respect to the origin at F in Fig. 8 (OF representing the given full-employment output of exportables) must be convex from above, and the offer curve is the locus of successive points of tangency of those curves with

[1] See Scitovsky's discussion of this point in [33].

the line of the terms of trade.[1] Each point represents then an equilibrium position with respect to the given terms of trade. The form of the offer curve may thus be expected to be similar to that of the locus of such points of tangency on a system of indifference curves of an individual consumer.

Strictly speaking these are not very compelling reasons for either the offer curve or a price-consumption curve to be bending upwards and then to the left. They are more intuitive than logical. As the two goods are important aggregates it is unlikely either for a country or for an individual consumer to give up either of them completely whatever the terms of trade. One might expect, therefore, that the greater are exports and the smaller is consumption of exportables, the weaker must be the substitution effect of any further fall in the price of importables. At some point the income effect should take over, and the offer curve should bend to the left. It is, however, also possible that it becomes vertical or even that it continues in the northeast direction until the whole output of exportables is sold abroad, provided only that at some very high price of the latter (in relation to that of importables) consumption of exportables is given up altogether in favour of importables. This would be a very unlikely situation. But it is not ruled out by any of the generally acceptable postulates of economic theory.

6

There is another, more subtle reason for imposing restrictions (though less severe than those discussed in the preceding section) on the form of the offer curves. It has been pointed out by Samuelson[2] that there is a correspondence of a sort between the conditions which must be satisfied for a model to tend to settle down to an equilibrium position (as determined by its parameters) and the form of the relations which determine the displacement of that equilibrium from one position to another

[1] This argument assumes complete specialisation. For a more detailed discussion of this point see Meade [16].
[2] [29] Chapter IX.

(when the parameters are changed). He showed how this correspondence may be used to determine the direction of the displacement of equilibrium, and he called the method of using it for this purpose the Correspondence Principle. Our task in this section is to see how this principle can be used to determine the direction of a displacement of equilibrium along an offer curve.

Let us return first to Fig. 8 and interpret the two offer curves as indicating the quantities of the two goods which the two countries demand and supply at different ratios of exchange. The curves presuppose such adjustments in the two economies as are necessary to keep exports and imports in balance. At point G the exchange ratio is in equilibrium because supply is equal to demand both for country H's exportables (OE) and for country H's importables (OM). Suppose, however, that the terms of trade line OT is less steep than that on the diagram. With the offer curves as they are, country H would then offer less exportables than the rest of the world would demand, and it would demand less importables than the rest of the world would offer. The tendency would thus be for the prices of exportables to increase, for those of importables to decrease, and for the terms of trade to improve towards the equilibrium position G. With all the adjustments of the rate of exchange, absorption, and wages, which the offer curves imply, the discrepancy between the quantities offered and demanded becomes smaller as the terms of trade improve, and it disappears altogether when the equilibrium position is reached. In this case, therefore, the model does tend towards the equilibrium position if it happens to be away from it.[1]

This is true as long as the rest of the world's offer curve Oq intersects the country H's offer curve OQ from left to right. At any terms-of-trade line less steep than OT the corresponding quantities of supply and demand on the former are then greater than those on the latter, and the argument of the preceding paragraph applies. If, however, Oq was turned downwards and

[1] This verbal analysis of stability glosses over many difficulties which only a more sophisticated mathematical treatment of the subject could reveal. This, however, would be outside the scope of the present book.

OQ to the left so that the former intersected the latter from right to left, the model would be unstable. It would tend to run further and further away from equilibrium if it happened not to be exactly at it. If thus we accept stability as a normal case (on the ground that after all we do not see in the real world the terms of trade running away in one direction or the other but rather hovering around some equilibrium level), we may invoke the Correspondence Principle to rule out the possibility of the offer curves intersecting in that way.

Fig. 9 represents the limiting case in which the offer curves do not intersect either one way or the other but coincide in the neighbourhood of G. It can be used to derive a rather neat algebraic condition for the unstable form of the curves to be ruled out. In the first place it can be shown that the elasticity of reciprocal demand in the neighbourhood of point P (any point on OQ) is equal to OB/OA if AH is tangential to the offer curve OQ at the point P.[1] For if we move from P an P' which is supposed to be very close to P, the proportional change in the quantity demanded is $P'R/P'N=SR/ON$, the proportional change in the price is SP/OB, and the elasticity of reciprocal demand is

$$\frac{SR}{SP} \cdot \frac{OB}{ON} = \frac{OB}{OA}$$

because $SR/SP=ON/OA$. If then this result is applied to OQ and Oq at the point G, it can be shown that in this particular case the elasticity of the former is KO/LO and that of the latter is LK/LO, the two adding up to unity. This is the required condition. For the terms of trade not to be running away from the equilibrium position the form of the offer curves must be such that the two elasticities of reciprocal demand around the equilibrium position add up to more than unity.[2] The condition looks exactly like that of a positive effect of devaluation on the balance of trade, expressed in (E). One difference, however,

---

[1] The proof outlined in this paragraph was given by Ożga in [23] p. 130. See also Lerner [10] p. 39.

[2] For a more advanced discussion of the application of the Correspondence Principle to the theory of international trade see Kemp [6] Chapter Five.

must not be overlooked. In (E) the elasticities are those of demand, in which we allow either for no changes in the parameters of the demand functions at all or for such changes in them as we think may accompany the change in the balance of trade which the formula predicts. In the present condition the elasticities are those of reciprocal demand, in which such changes in the parameters are allowed for as are necessary to maintain equilibrium of the balance of trade. Thus in spite of identical form the content of the two conditions is different.

7

The offer curve analysis does not throw any more light on the factors which determine the terms of trade than the supply and demand analysis does. It helps only to put the movements along the supply and demand curves and some of the shifts of those curves together, and to formulate some plausible generalisations about the effect on the terms of trade of disturbances in the conditions on which they depend.

The disturbance which we will find useful to consider in this section is that of unilateral payments abroad. This is the so called transfer problem. It assumed a considerable importance after the First World War when Germany accepted responsibility for large sums of money to be paid to the victorious countries as reparations. The question then arose whether in addition to the sums to be transferred the paying country had to carry also a burden due to unfavourable change in the terms of trade. Nowadays the question is much less topical than it was at that time. We will see, however, in the last section of this chapter that the analysis of the transfer problem may throw additional light on the relation between exchange rate adjustments on one hand and the balance of payments and the terms of trade on the other.

To deal with these matters by means of the offer-curve technique, the concept of an offer curve must be generalised so as to make it independent of the assumption of the zero balance of trade. It has been pointed out already that the latter is only a special case of the assumption of a given balance of trade. To consider a situation corresponding to this more general assumption suppose thus that trade in Fig. 8 is not balanced, but that there is a surplus in country H equal to OR in terms of home-produced goods. It follows that with national income equal to OF absorption in terms of home-produced goods in country H must be equal to RF. An offer curve RQ' may then be drawn which shows how much of foreign goods country H would demand at various terms of trade and how much (in terms of home-produced goods) she would be prepared to pay for them, assuming that absorption in terms of home-produced goods remains equal to RF. Similarly an offer curve may be drawn for the rest of the world W on the assumption that the deficit of the balance of trade there is given and equal to OR' and absorption is $R'F'$ (both in terms of the goods produced in the rest of the world). In Fig. 8 it is represented by Rq'.

The technique of the offer curves generalised in this way may now be used to analyse the transfer problem.[1] Reparations may be represented in Fig. 8 by OR. They lead to a rightward shift of the offer curve OQ. For if, for instance, OR of country H's coal is to be sent abroad as reparations, absorption in terms of country H's exportables must be reduced to RF, and the surplus of the balance of trade is OR. The offer curve of the rest of the world also shifts to the right. For to absorb OR of country H's goods received as reparations, the amount of absorption in the rest of the world must increase to $R'P'$ in terms of W's exportables, and there appears a deficit of the balance of trade there, equal to OR'. As reparations are free, the balance of payments remains in equilibrium. The argument applies, of course, also to those cases in which the transfer is due not to reparations but to credits granted abroad or to accumulation of gold and foreign exchange reserves in country H. Transfer may here be understood as simply another word for

[1] For a more detailed discussion of how the offer-curve technique can be applied to problems of the balance of payments see Meade [16] and [17]. A more extensive textbook treatment of the transfer problem may be found in Haberler [4], Chapter VII and VIII, and in Kindleberger [8], Chapter 18. Compare also contemporary contributions by Keynes [7] and Ohlin [21].

a change in the given deficit or surplus of the balance of trade.

The conditions for the terms of trade to remain unaffected by such a change in the balance of trade is that the two curves intersect now at some point G' on the terms-of-trade line RT' parallel to OT. This means that as a result of the transfer country H has reduced its consumption of importables and of exportables by exactly the same amounts as the rest of the world has increased it. In other words the same proportion of the change in absorption (decrease in country H and increase in the rest of the world W) must be spent there on the two aggregates of goods ($KG'/OR=KL/OR'$ on H's exportables and $KG/OR'=SK/OR$ on W's exportables). The respective proportions are marginal propensities to import and to consume exportables respectively. The condition for the terms of trade to remain unchanged is thus that the marginal propensities to import in country H ($SK/OR=GK/OR'$) and in the rest of the world W ($KG'/OR=KL/OR'$) add up to unity. If they add up to less than unity, that is to say if the reduction in demand for importables in country H is less than the increase in demand for them in the rest of the world W, and the reduction in demand in country H for its own exportables is greater than the increase in demand for them in the rest of the world, the offer curve OQ' must intersect the RT' line above the point at which RT' is intersected by Oq', and (if the curves have the form as on the diagram) the terms of trade must move against country H. If the marginal propensities to import add up to more than unity, the terms of trade improve. It is often argued that as in addition to exportables and importables there are also domestic goods (which, if aggregation is on the ground of substitutability on the side of production, are often put together with exportables into one aggregate of home-produced goods), the marginal propensities to import are more likely to add up to less than unity, and a deterioration of the terms of trade is more probable than an improvement. The condition, however, that the form of the offer curves is as on the diagram must not be overlooked. For if the sum of their elasticities at the point of intersection were less than unity, that is to say that if Oq intersected OQ

from right to left, the conditions for a favourable and an unfavourable adjustment in the terms of trade would be just the other way round.

8

The argument may now be put into reverse to throw more light on the effect of exchange rate adjustments as a means of improving the balance of payments.[1] In the preceding section the adjustments in the rate of exchange were regarded as a possible concomitant of the transfer and of the corresponding change in the terms of trade. For a change in the terms of trade could there take place only if there was a change in either the price of the aggregate of home-produced goods or in the rate of exchange. A change in the latter was, therefore, an effect of a sort of the transfer if the conditions of internal balance were to be maintained. It is possible, however, to look at these adjustments from a different point of view. Suppose that a given surplus of the balance of trade is required to put the balance of payments in equilibrium and stop the drain on the reserves. By what adjustments in the rate of exchange can this be brought about?

The question has been already considered in Chapter V. The technique of the offer curves, however, allows us to deal with it in a slightly different way and (as we will see in a while) with slightly different results. For let us put the question as at the end of the preceding paragraph. We may then argue that in order to arrive at the balance of trade surplus equal to OR in Fig. 8 country H must reduce absorption in terms of home-produced goods from OF to RF and adjust the terms of trade from OT to OT'; and that in order to achieve this latter objective and yet leave the price level of home-produced goods unchanged it has to adjust the rate of exchange exactly in the same proportion. If RT' happens to be steeper than OT, the currency of country H has to be appreciated; if RT' happens to be less steep, the currency must be depreciated. It has been shown, however, in the preceding section that whether RT' is steeper or less steep than OT depends on whether the sum of

---

[1] Compare the treatment of this subject by Samuelson [32].

the marginal propensities to import in country H and in the rest of the world W is greater or less than unity. (Provided always that the offer curves intersect as on the diagram, i.e. that the sum of the elasticities of demand they embody is greater than unity. If the sum of the elasticities was less than unity, the condition about the sum of the marginal propensities to import would have to be reversed.) Thus we have arrived at a conclusion which seems to be completely at variance with what was established before. According to formula (E), which too corresponds to the case of constant prices of home-produced goods, depreciation of the currency improves the balance of trade if the sum of the elasticities of demand for imports is greater than unity; and according to the result established now, it improves the balance of trade if the sum of the marginal propensities to import is less than unity.

The paradox is due to a trick which the *ceteris paribus* clause can play on us if we give it more scope than there is room for it. In formula (E) the elasticities of demand are subject to the *ceteris paribus* clause. The demand relations from which they derive (and which determine the flow of trade) are either supposed to be independent of whatever changes in absorption may take place or they subsume those changes already in their form. The elasticities embodied in the offer curves are not subject to this condition. As absorption is reduced in country H and increased in W, both offer curves shift to the right and very likely change their form. And this change in the form of the curves is as relevant to the adjustments in the flow of trade as the movements along the curves which the elasticities describe.

To see how relevant it is suppose that as the offer curves in Fig. 8 shift to the right no change in their form takes place. This corresponds to the case in which the demand relations from which the elasticities in (E) are derived are independent of whatever adjustments in absorption are required to keep the economy in internal balance (identified with constant prices of home-produced goods). Thus country H's offer curve shifts to the right point by point by a distance equal to OR, and the rest of the world's curve shifts downwards, also point by point until it passes through R. Suppose further that RT' is not a new line of terms of trade but simply a parallel to OT. It is then clear that country H's offer curve after the shift (not drawn on the diagram) must cut that line at V, and it must be below RT' over its whole length between R and V. The new offer curve of the rest of the world, on the other hand, must cut RT' below L and be below that line further to the right. Thus the two offer curves would intersect somewhere below RT', to the right of L and to the left of V. In this case, therefore, the condition that the sum of the two elasticities of demand is greater than unity, i.e. that country H's offer curve intersects the rest of the world's curve from left to right, is a sufficient condition for a depreciation of country H's currency to have a favourable effect on the balance of trade. If the sum of the two elasticities was less than unity and the two curves intersected the other way round, they would intersect above RT' after the shift, and the currency of country H would have to be appreciated for the balance of trade to improve.

It is easy to see that this result is not inconsistent with the condition established at the beginning of this section. For a parallel shift of an offer curve means that the whole increase in absorption is spent on home-produced goods and the marginal propensity to import is zero. The sum of the two propensities is thus also zero, always less than unity. This is what is implied in formula (E) if the conditions of demand which its elasticities summarize are supposed to be independent of whatever happens to absorption. If they summarize also the shifts in the demand relations due to possible changes in absorption, the numerical value of their sum depends already on whether the marginal propensities to import add up to more or less than unity, and no additional condition is required. In that case, however, the elasticities are merely descriptions of the actual behaviour of exports and imports, and as has been already pointed out in the preceding chapter, they do not tell us anything about the relations on which this behaviour depends.[1]

[1] The argument of this section has been strongly influenced by Pearce's treatment of this topic in [25], and a reader who is interested in more advanced analysis is advised to consider this reference very carefully.

VII

Continuous Adjustments

In the preceding chapters the stress was on the factors which determine the terms of trade and the rate of exchange. The basic assumption was that of equilibrium, either partial or general, according to what the particular model required. The relations which the analysis attempted to elucidate were those which determined that equilibrium, the terms of trade and the rate of exchange being one of the characteristics of it.

This method has also been developed along the lines of comparative statistics. Suppose that a particular change occurs in the conditions of supply or of demand for exports or for imports. Let, for instance, autonomous investment increase, or let the autonomous items in the balance of payments change in a particular way. What effect may this have on the terms of trade and on the rate of exchange? It is to answer questions like those that the whole equilibrium theory of international trade has been devised. What changes in the supply and demand conditions actually occur is beside the point. The analysis applies equally well to shock changes in the parameters and once-for-all adjustments to them, as to continuous displacements of equilibrium due to development and growth.

In this last chapter the method of comparative statics will be applied to continuous displacements only. What tendencies in the balance of payments may appear as a result of a continuous growth of the economies concerned, and to what adjustments in the rate of exchange may they lead? No conclusive answer to this question can be given with respect to all aspects of change which economic growth implies. Not much theoretical work has in fact been done along these lines.[1] Only, therefore, one or two aspects of the theory will be developed here, more to give an illustration of the problems with which a growth theory of international trade is concerned and of the relations which it allows us to establish, than to cover the field.

1

Two general points have to be made at the beginning. One is about the dynamic character of the analysis; the other is about the conditions of external and internal balance on which the analysis depends.

The theory of economic growth is dynamic economics. Like all dynamics it deals with changes over time, determined by intertemporal relations between its variables. A change in income, for instance, determines the change in capital stock, which in turn determines the change in income. But in the growth theory of international trade (such as has been developed so far and is going to be outlined here) no intertemporal relations are incorporated into the model. The change occurs in the data and is supposed to be exogenously given. For one must remember that what is a variable in a general growth model may be a parameter in an international trade model. If, for instance, the purpose of the latter is to explain how trade tends to adjust itself to growth of aggregate outputs in the countries concerned, the outputs are parameters in the model of trade; and they are endogenous variables in a general model of economic growth.

It is precisely with this type of adjustment that we will deal in the present chapter. The endogenous variables of trade adjust themselves to exogenously given changes in the parameters on which they depend. Although, therefore, the analysis deals with changes over time, the method is in fact that of comparative statics. There is only this qualification that the displacements

[1] Johnson [5], Chapter III, J. Black [2] and Ramaswami [27] may be recommended as supplementary reading. A survey of other contributors in this field may also be found in Caves [3], Chapter IX.

of equilibrium are continuous, due to continuous changes in data.

With respect to internal and external balance, it must be emphasised that a theory of balance of payments adjustments is a short-run theory. So is an international trade theory of income determination with unemployed resources. Over long periods of time there cannot be any disequilibrium of the balance of payments. Nor is there any need to allow in our analysis for unemployment of scarce productive resources.[1] Some mechanism always exists for temporary deviations from equilibrium to be corrected. On the average economies must always be in internal and in external balance. A growth theory of the rate of exchange and of the terms of trade deals, therefore, with two general questions only. What adjustments in the rate of exchange are required to maintain external balance, assuming that the conditions of internal balance are satisfied throughout? And what adjustments in the terms of trade do the conditions of internal and external balance imply?

These are the questions which will be considered in more detail in the present chapter. To be able, however, to say what adjustments in the rates of exchange and in the terms of trade economic growth may require, we must consider first the potential trends in the balance of trade which these adjustments may be called forth to correct.

2

To deal with these preliminary matters we must return first to the one-commodity model which was introduced in Chapter IV. Suppose that all goods and services produced in country H and in the rest of the world W are treated as two aggregates, and that the prices of those aggregates are constant. This is how the condition of internal balance is supposed to be maintained. Suppose also that the rate of exchange remains unchanged. Identity (A) tells us then that the terms of trade also remain

---

[1] This does not exclude the possibility of unemployment of either labour or land in under-developed countries in which these resources are not scarce.

83

unchanged. And this means that all goods in the model can be added or subtracted, one to or from another, at a constant ratio of prices. In spite of there being two aggregates, the model is in fact a one-community one.

In accordance with the assumption of full employment which was made in the preceding section, no allowance can be made here for any spare capacity. Income in real terms is determined by the available productive resources and can change only if these resources change. Suppose that in the initial position the balance of trade is in equilibrium, absorption in real terms being equal to real income. And let the element of growth be introduced by making the latter grow at some given rate. The rate may be different in country H from that in the rest of the world W. The assumption is only that in either case it is given exogenously. Is it possible for the balance of trade to remain in equilibrium as growth at these rates proceeds? The following conditions may be formulated in terms of income elasticities of demand for imports and of marginal propensities to import for the answer to be positive.

With respect to marginal propensities to import the argument is as follows. The change in imports in country H is

$$\Delta M = m_h \Delta A$$

and the change in exports is

$$\Delta E = m_w \Delta a$$

where (as in the previous chapters) ΔA, Δa are absolute changes in absorption, and m_h, m_w the marginal propensities to import, in country H and in the rest of the world W respectively. Bearing in mind that if the balance of trade is in equilibrium aggregate income is equal to absorption, the condition of equilibrium of the balance of trade may be written as

$$\Delta M = \Delta E = {}_{mh}\Delta Y = m_w \Delta y$$

or
$$\frac{\Delta Y}{\Delta y} = \frac{m_w}{m_h} \tag{F}$$

where ΔY and Δy are absolute changes in real income in H and in W.

This is the required condition in terms of marginal propensities to import. For the balance of trade to remain in equilibrium the absolute increments of Y and of y must be inversely proportional to the respective marginal propensities to import. To obtain the condition in terms of income elasticities of demand for imports both sides of $m_h\Delta Y=m_w\Delta y$ have to be divided by $M=E$ and multiplied by $A/Y=a/y=1$. We obtain then

$$\left(\frac{\Delta M}{\Delta A}\cdot\frac{A}{M}\right)\left(\frac{\Delta Y}{Y}\right) = \left(\frac{\Delta E}{\Delta a}\cdot\frac{a}{E}\right)\left(\frac{\Delta y}{y}\right)$$

or
$$\frac{\theta_h}{\theta_w} = \frac{G_w}{G_h} \qquad\qquad (G)$$

where θ_h, θ_w are income elasticities of demand for imports and G_h, G_w are the given rates of growth of real income in country H and in the rest of the world respectively. The formula says that for the balance of trade to remain in equilibrium the rates of growth G_h and G_w must be inversely proportional to the respective income elasticities of demand for imports. If, as in Chapter IV, a constant proportion of absorption is always spent on imports, $\theta_h=\theta_w=1$, and the formula reduces to

$$G_w = G_h \qquad\qquad (H)$$

In this special case the two rates of growth must thus be equal one to the other.[1]

3

The argument may be illustrated geometrically by means of Fig. 10, which has been constructed along the same lines as Fig. 6. If the balance of trade is in equilibrium, the relation between absorption and national income must correspond to the 45° line in the first quadrant for country H and in the third quadrant for the rest of the world W. For equilibrium of the balance of trade implies that absorption is and remains equal to aggregate income. Thus OY and oy represent both income and absorption in H and in W. If then OU is the relation between

[1] These conditions were originally formulated by Johnson [5] p. 139/140.

absorption and imports in country H, its slope with respect to the vertical axis is the marginal propensity to import in H. Similarly the slope of Ou is the marginal propensity to import in the rest of the world. The condition that the balance of trade is in equilibrium can then be written as $OE=OM$ and $EE'=MM'$. With the given slopes of OU and Ou this imposes a definite restriction on the relation between the two increments YY' and yy', the same restriction in fact which appears in (F). If it is not satisfied, the whole model must break down. For the appearance of á surplus or of a deficit in the balance of trade would then mean that absorption is no longer equal to national income, and the 45° relations in the first and the third quadrant of the diagram no longer apply.

4

The argument can be developed so as to cover also the case in which the balance of trade is not in equilibrium but ratio b remains constant. Suppose that initially imports are greater than exports, and that the difference between them is equal to YA. Absorption in country H is OA, and imports are Om. Similarly absorption in W is Oa, and the country H's exports are Oe. Let then income in H and in W increase to OY' and Oy' respectively, absorption to OA' and Oa', and imports and exports to Om' and Oe'. What conditions must be satisfied for the balance of trade ratio b to remain unchanged in the course of this process?

If constant proportions of absorption are always spent on imports, the answer is quite straightforward. A constant ratio b means that both exports and imports are growing at the same proportional rate. Thus the condition is that

$$\frac{mm'}{Om} = \frac{ee'}{Oe} = \frac{mm'-ee'}{Om-Oe}$$

and the deficit of the balance of trade is also growing at that rate. With OU and Ou being straight lines drawn through the origin, the above condition implies

$$\frac{AA'}{OA} = \frac{aa'}{Oa} = \frac{Y'A'-YA}{YA} = \frac{y'a'-ya}{ya}$$

Hence,

$$G_h = \frac{YY'}{OY'} = \frac{AA'-Y'A'+YA}{OA-YA} = \frac{aa'+y'a'-ya}{Oa+ya} = \frac{y'y}{Oy} = G_w$$

Condition (H), derived as a special case of (G), is still valid. As long as both income elasticities of demand for imports are equal to unity, equality of the proportional rates of growth is a necessary (and sufficient) condition for the ratio b to remain constant, irrespective of whether b is or is not equal to unity.

The case in which the proportions of absorption spent on imports are not constant (i.e. $\theta_h \neq 1$, $\theta_w \neq 1$) is a little more complicated. If OU and Ou are not straight lines passing through the origin, the equalities written in the preceding paragraph no longer hold. We may, however, still write

$$AA' = \frac{mm'}{m_h} = YY'+mm'-ee'$$

Bearing in mind that $ee'=b.mm'$ and denoting YY' by ΔY, we have

$$m_h\Delta Y = mm'[1-m_h(1-b)]$$

Similarly,

$$aa' = \frac{ee'}{m_w} = yy' - mm'+ee'$$

and

$$m_w\Delta y = mm'[b+m_w(1-b)]$$

Dividing one through the other we obtain

$$\frac{m_h\Delta Y}{m_w\Delta y} = \frac{1-m_h(1-b)}{b+m_w(1-b)} \tag{I}$$

Condition (F) appears now as a special case of (I), that in which b is equal to unity.

To obtain the condition in terms of income elasticities of demand multiply the numerator of (I) by A/MY, the denominator by a/Ey, and substitute θ's and G's for income elasticities of demand for imports and for the proportional rates of growth of income respectively. We can then write

$$\frac{\theta_h G_h}{\theta_w G_w}=\frac{E}{M}\cdot\frac{\dfrac{A}{Y}-\dfrac{M}{Y}(1-b)\theta_h}{\dfrac{ba}{y}+\dfrac{bM}{y}(1-b)\theta_w}$$

If then we cancel E/M with b and substitute $-B$ (country H's deficit, i.e. negative surplus, of the balance of trade) for $M(1-b)$, $Y-B$ for A, and $y+B$ for a, we obtain

$$\frac{\theta_h G_h}{\theta_w G_h}=\frac{1-\beta_h(1-\theta_h)}{1+\beta_w(1-\theta_w)} \tag{J}$$

where β_h and β_w are the ratios B/Y and B/y respectively. The results obtained before, (G) and (H), may now be derived as special cases of (J); the former corresponding to $\beta_h=\beta_w=0$, and the latter to $\theta_h=\theta_w=1$.

5

Having established the conditions in which the balance of trade ratio remains constant, we may now turn to the case in which these conditions are not satisfied. As a result of the economies of country H and of the rest of the world W growing at their respective rates, there is then a tendency for the balance of trade ratio to change. If originally trade was balanced, a deficit or a surplus tends to appear, and it tends to grow bigger and bigger at an ever increasing rate. It has been already pointed out in the first section of this chapter that such tendencies cannot continue over long periods of time. Sooner or later disequilibrium must be corrected either by suitable changes in absorption, income, and the general price level, or by adjustments in the rate of exchange. In the present model the first possibility is ruled out by the assumption of internal balance. What, therefore, has to be considered is the second possibility only. What adjustments in the rate of exchange have to take place for the balance of trade ratio to remain constant when condition (J) is not satisfied?

The argument consists in bringing together the least complicated parts of the analysis presented in the preceding sections of this chapter and in Chapter V. The least complicated parts only have to be brought together because the conditions of the model do not admit anything more involved. In the first place, the condition that the countries concerned are and remain in external balance precludes the possibility of the balance of trade ratio b being different from unity. This disposes of all the complications which had to be taken into account when moving from (G) to (J). In the second place, the condition that all goods produced in a country are treated as one aggregate and the assumption of internal balance dispose of many of the complications which had to be taken into account in Chapter V. It is true that as soon as the rate of exchange is allowed to vary our one-commodity model turns into a two-commodity one. For the goods produced in one country cannot be converted in that case into those produced in the other country at a constant ratio of prices. Demand for imports depends then no only on the amount of absorption but also on the rate of exchange, i.e. on the price of imports. As long, however, as importables are not produced in the importing country, the assumption of internal balance may be identified with that of perfectly elastic curves of supply of exports.[1]

6

The ground having been so thoroughly cleared of all unnecessary obstacles the analysis may now be given in a few lines. With absorption growing in H and W, and with a variable rate of exchange, any change in the balance of trade may be split into two parts. One is the change due to the growth of absorption, the rate of exchange being constant; the other is the change due to the adjustment of the rate of exchange, absorption being constant. With $b=1$ the rate of growth of absorption is equal to the exogenously given rate of growth of income. By a suitable adjustment of units in the initial position one unit of exports may be made equal in value (in terms of foreign currency) to

---

[1] See Section 4 of Chapter V.

one unit of imports, and the condition for the overall change of the balance of trade to vanish may be written as follows:

$$\frac{\Delta B}{M} = \left[\theta_w G_w - \theta_h G_h\right] + \left[(\varepsilon_e + \varepsilon_m - 1)\frac{\Delta r}{r}\right] = 0$$

The element in the first squared bracket on the right-hand side represents the change due to the growth of absorption, taken over from (G); the element in the second squared bracket represents the change due to the adjustment in the rate of exchange, taken over from (E) in Chapter V; and the condition of external balance is satisfied if these two elements just cancel out.[1] We obtain, therefore, the following solution for the adjustment in the rate of exchange

$$G_r = \frac{\Delta r}{r} = \frac{\theta_h G_h - \theta_w G_w}{(\varepsilon_m + \varepsilon_e) - 1} \tag{K}$$

It tells us that if $\varepsilon_m + \varepsilon_e > 1$, that is to say if the adjustments in the rate of exchange brought about by the pressures of supply and demand for foreign exchange have really an equilibrating influence on the latter, the direction of those adjustments depends on the sign of the difference between the products of the income elasticity of demand for imports and the rate of growth, in country H and in the rest of the world respectively.[2] If this difference is equal to zero, there is no adjustment in the rate of exchange, and we are back at (G).

7

How do the terms of trade behave in the course of the process of growth described above? The answer is quite straightforward. In the model of this chapter they behave in exactly the same way as the rate of exchange does. For so far it has been assumed

[1] The reader, however, must be reminded of the limitations of (E) which were discussed in Section 4 of Chapter V and in 8 of Chapter VI. Unless the conditions of *ceteris paribus* are satisfied with respect to the supply and demand relations for imports and exports, the elasticity coefficients ε_m and ε_e describe in fact not the demand relations but the actual behaviour of exports and imports, brought about by a change in all the parameters which appear in those relations.

[2] This is again Johnson's formula, see [5] p. 141.

throughout that money prices of the two aggregates remain constant. This has been one of the conditions of internal balance. Thus both sides of identity (A) remain constant, and the terms of trade T change in the same proportion as the rate of exchange r does. We may thus write

$$G_T = \frac{\Delta T}{T} = \frac{\theta_h G_h - \theta_w G_w}{(\varepsilon_m + \varepsilon_e) - 1} \tag{L}$$

in accordance with (K). The conclusion derives simply from the basic assumption about the degree of aggregation.

This result may now be used to turn the question back on the rate of exchange and to show how the latter would behave if the money prices of the aggregates do not remain constant. For it has been explained in Chapter VI by means of Fig. 8 that in the conditions of external and internal balance the terms of trade may be derived from the offer curves through identity (B), quite independently of how money prices and the rate of exchange happen to behave. If, therefore, the terms of trade satisfy (L) in the conditions of constant money prices and of the rate of exchange behaving according to (K), they must also satisfy it if money prices are not constant and the rate of exchange behaves in some other way. Identity (A) may then be used to answer the question. In terms of the proportional rates of change of the four variables which appear in it, it can be written as

$$G_T - G_r = G_p - GP$$

Substituting from (L) we then obtain

$$G_r = \frac{\theta_h G_h - \theta_w G_w}{(\varepsilon_m + \varepsilon_e) - 1} + (GP - G_p) \tag{M}$$

Thus the behaviour of the rate of exchange depends on the behaviour of real incomes and of the price levels in H and in W, the elasticities θ_h, θ_w, ε_m and ε_e being the parameters which fix the relation.

The way in which (M) has been written suggests that G_r is a dependent variable, determined by all the others as data. However, this need not be so. Stable exchange rates may be an essential objective of economic policy, and it is through suitable adjustments in the terms on the right-hand side of (M) that it is meant to be achieved. In fact, policy objectives include usually some restrictions on all G's in (M), and the problem is how to adjust the parameters which fix the relations between them, so as to make them compatible one with another.

Diagrams

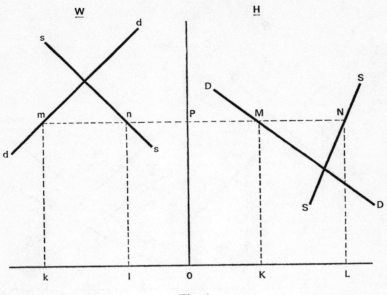

Fig. 1

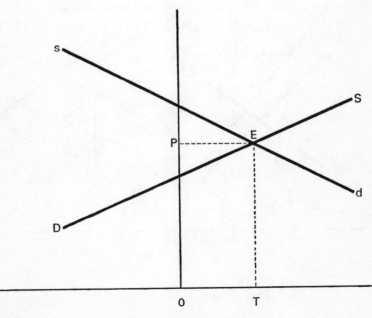

Fig. 2

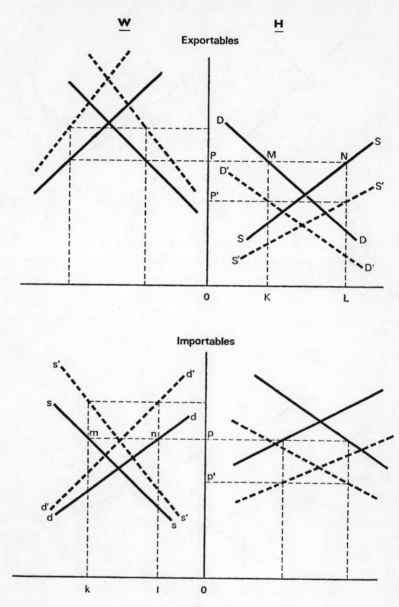

Fig. 3

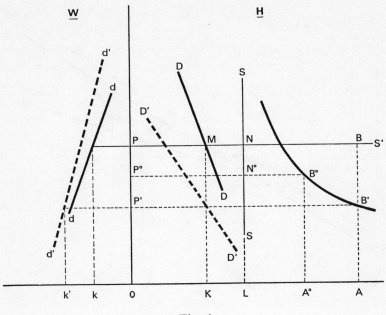

Fig. 4

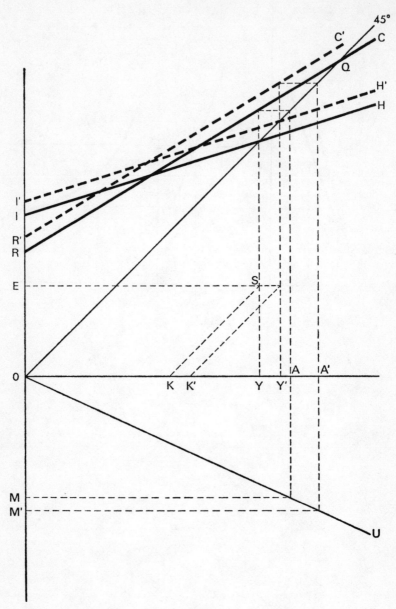

Fig. 5

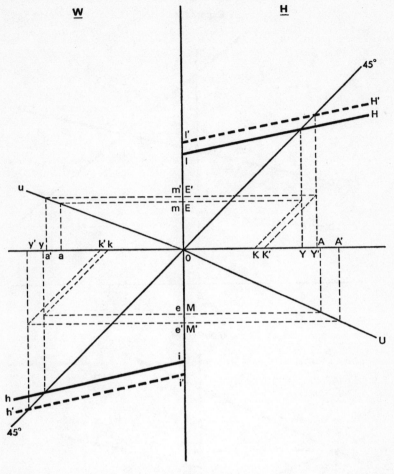

Fig. 6

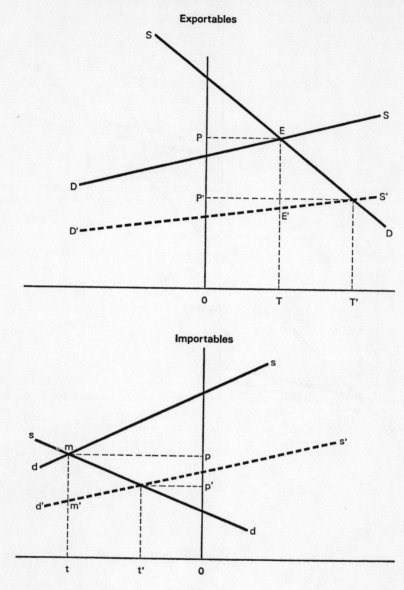

Fig. 7

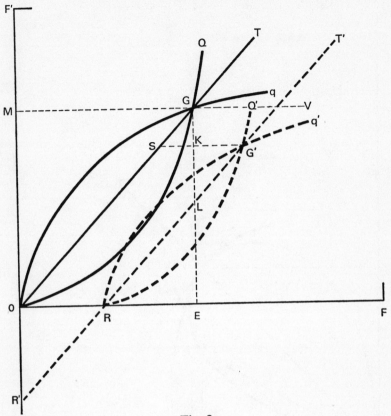

Fig. 8

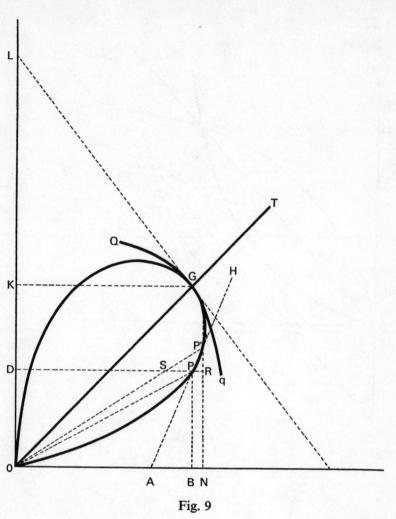

Fig. 9

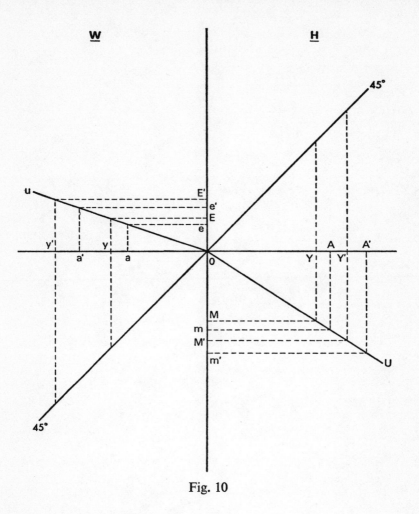

Fig. 10

Basic Formulae

$$\frac{T}{r} \equiv \frac{p}{p} \tag{A}$$

$$Tb \equiv \frac{E}{M} \tag{B}$$

$$\begin{aligned} D_e &= D_e\,(P, rp, A) \\ D_m &= D_m\,(P, rp, A) \end{aligned} \tag{C}$$

$$\begin{aligned} S_e &= S_e\,(P, w) \\ S_m &= S_m\,(rp, w) \\ S_d &= S_d\,(\pi, w) \end{aligned} \tag{D}$$

$$\frac{\Delta B}{M} = \left(\varepsilon_e + \varepsilon_m - 1\right) \frac{\Delta r}{r} \tag{E}$$

$$\frac{\Delta Y}{\Delta y} = \frac{m_w}{m_h} \tag{F}$$

$$\frac{\theta_h}{\theta_w} = \frac{G_w}{G_h} \tag{G}$$

$$G_w = G_h \tag{H}$$

$$\frac{m_h \Delta Y}{m_w \Delta y} = \frac{1 - m_h\,(1-b)}{b + m_w(1-b)} \tag{I}$$

$$\frac{\theta_h G_h}{\theta_w G_w} = \frac{1 - \beta_h(1-\theta_h)}{1 + \beta_w(1-\theta_w)} \tag{J}$$

$$G_r = \frac{\Delta r}{r} = \frac{\theta_h G_h - \theta_w G_w}{(\theta_m + \theta_e) - 1} \tag{K}$$

$$G_T = \frac{\Delta T}{T} = \frac{\theta_h G_h - \theta_w G_w}{(\varepsilon_m + \varepsilon_e) - 1} \tag{L}$$

$$G_r = \frac{\theta_h G_h - \theta_w G_w}{(\varepsilon_m + \varepsilon_e) - 1} + (GP - G_p) \tag{M}$$

105

Bibliography

Bibliography

[1] SIDNEY S. ALEXANDER, 'Effects of a Devaluation on a Trade Balance', *IMF Staff Papers*, Vol. II, April 1952.

[2] J. BLACK, 'Economic Expansion and International Trade: A Marshallian Approach', *Review of Economic Studies*, Vol. XXIII, 1955–6.

[3] RICHARD E. CAVES, *Trade and Economic Structure*, Harvard University Press, 1963.

[4] GOTTFRIED VON HABERLER, *The Theory of International Trade* (English Translation), William Hodge, 1950.

[5] HARRY G. JOHNSON, *International Trade and Economic Growth*, Allen and Unwin, 1958.

[6] MURRAY C. KEMP, *The Pure Theory of International Trade*, Prentice-Hall, 1964.

[7] J.M. KEYNES, 'The German Transfer Problem', *Economic Journal*, Vol. XXXIX, March 1929.

[8] CHARLES P. KINDLEBERGER, *International Economics*, Irwin, 1963.

[9] WASSILY W. LEONTIEF, 'The Use of Indifference Curves in the Analysis of Foreign Trade', *Quarterly Journal of Economics*, Vol. XLVII, May 1933.

[10] A.P. LERNER, 'The Diagrammatical Representation of Elasticity of Demand', *Review of Economic Studies*, Vol. 1, October 1933.

[11] A.P. LERNER, 'The Symmetry between Import and Export Taxes', *Economica*, N.S. Vol. III, August 1936.

[12] RICHARD G. LIPSEY, 'The Theory of Customs Unions: Trade Diversion and Welfare', *Economica*, N.S. Vol. XXIV, February 1957.

[13] FRITZ MACHLUP, 'Relative Prices and Aggregate Spending in the Analysis of Devaluation', *American Economic Review*, Vol. XLV, June 1955.

[14] FRITZ MACHLUP, 'The Theory of Foreign Exchanges', *Economica*, N.S. Vol. VI, November 1939.

[15] ALRED MARSHALL, *The Pure Theory of Foreign Trade*, London School of Economics, 1930.

[16] JAMES EDWARD MEADE, '*A Geometry of International Trade*', Allen and Unwin, 1952.

[17] J.E. MEADE, 'A Geometrical Representation of Balance of Payments Policy', *Economica*, N.S. Vol. XVI, November 1949.

[18] J.E. MEADE, *The Theory of International Economic Policy: The Balance of Payments*, Oxford University Press, 1951.

[19] J.E. MEADE, *The Theory of International Economic Policy: Trade and Welfare*, Oxford University Press, 1955.

[20] JOHN STUART MILL, *Principles of Political Economy*, Longmans, 1940.

[21] BERTIL OHLIN, 'The Reparation Problem: A Discussion', *Economic Journal*, Vol. XXXIX, June 1929.

[22] S.A. OŻGA, 'An Essay in the Theory of Tariffs', *Journal of Political Economy*, Vol. LXIII, December 1955.

[23] S.A. OŻGA, 'A Note on the Geometrical Representation of Elasticity of Demand for Imports', *Economica*, N.S. Vol. XX, May 1953.

[24] S.A. OŻGA, 'Tariffs and the Balance of Payments', *Quarterly Journal of Economics*, Vol. LXXI, November 1957.

[25] I.F. PEARCE, 'The Problem of the Balance of Payments', *International Economic Review*, Vol. 2, January 1961.

[26] I.F. PEARCE, and S.F. JAMES, 'The Factor Price Equalisation Myth', *Review of Economic Studies*, Vol. XIX, 1951–2.

[27] V.K. RAMASWAMI, 'The Effects of Accumulation on the Terms of Trade', *Economic Journal*, Vol. LXX, September 1960.

[28] JOAN ROBINSON, *Essays in the Theory of Employment*, Blackwell, 1947.

[29] PAUL ANTHONY SAMUELSON, *Foundations of Economic Analysis*, Harvard University Press, 1947.

[30] PAUL A. SAMUELSON, 'International Trade and Equalisation of Factor Prices', *Economic Journal*, Vol. LVIII, June 1948.

[31] PAUL A. SAMUELSON, 'International Factor Price Equalisation Once Again', *Economic Journal*, Vol. LIX, June 1949.

[32] PAUL A. SAMUELSON, 'The Transfer Problem and Transport Costs', *Economic Journal*, Vol. LXII, June 1952, and Vol. LXIV, June 1954.

[33] T. DE SCITOVSKY, 'A Reconsideration of the Theory of Tariffs', *Review of Economic Studies*, Vol. IX, Summer 1942.

[34] WOLFGANG F. STOLPER and PAUL A. SAMUELSON, 'Protection and Real Wages', *Review of Economic Studies*, Vol. IX, November 1941.

[35] JAROSLAV VANEK, *International Trade*, Irwin, 1962.

[36] JACOB VINER, *The Customs Union Issue*, Stevens, 1950.

[37] JACOB VINER, *Studies in the Theory of International Trade*, Harper, 1937.

Index

Index